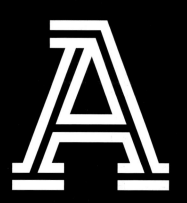

Contents

Introduction

Bringing It Home

By Sean Gentille

Midway through the third period, you'll hear it — and if you're at Ball Arena, you won't be able to hear much else.

"All the / small things / true care / truth brings ..."

This is how it's worked at Avalanche games when the home side is leading since the fall of 2019, when Craig "DJ Triple T" Turney decided to add the Blink-182 staple "All the Small Things" to the in-arena mix. Not long after, it became an Avalanche staple, too. And now, nearly three years later, it's the theme song for a Stanley Cup run.

The Avalanche — five seasons after finishing in last place in the league with a 21-point buffer — are the champions of the NHL. Their reputation as a regular-season-only phenomenon is in the rearview. Sometime soon, they'll start thinking bigger. How could they not? That's what you do when you've got foundational stars, locked-in role players, a front office that knows what it wants and a coaching staff that knows how to blend it all together. That's what you do when you're the real deal. That's what you do when you have dynasty potential.

Those are plans for later days, though. Now, the sound of a 20,000-member collective singing at the top of its register is still hanging in the Colorado atmosphere. You see, the DJ never plays the full song. When play resumes, the guitars cut out and we're left with an a cappella show.

"Say it ain't so, I will not go / Turn the lights off, carry me home ..."

Well, the Avalanche are home. And they beat the Tampa Bay Lightning — two-time defending champs and a mini-dynasty in their own right — to the door.

Though the route to the franchise's third Stanley Cup championship was by no means easy, the Avalanche made it look that way at times. Their 16-4 playoff record stands among the great postseasons in NHL history.

The path to the Stanley Cup, of course, was far longer than a 20-game playoff run. It started in the summer of 2011, when Joe Sakic rejoined the organization he'd led, as a captain and future Hall of Famer, to titles in 1996 and 2001.

In Sakic's first offseason with the front office, the Avs drafted Swedish winger Gabriel Landeskog at No. 2. Landeskog is 29 now, a 30-goal scorer in his 10th season as Colorado's captain. He's the connective tissue between the franchise's initial rebuild and the moment he took the Cup from NHL deputy commissioner Bill Daly as Sakic looked on.

Nathan MacKinnon came along two years after Landeskog, the first pick of the draft after a 16-win lockout-shortened season. On his best days, MacKinnon is one of the greatest hockey players on Earth — a rare combination of speed, skill and drive.

Only five skaters in the history of the NHL have averaged more points per playoff game than MacKinnon.

Not far behind MacKinnon on that list is Mikko Rantanen. The playmaking winger, taken with the 10th pick in 2015, was Colorado's leading scorer in 2021-22, with 92 points in the regular season. That a player of his caliber manages to fly under the radar — he led the Avs with 36 goals, too — might be the best testament to what Sakic and company have built in Colorado.

Two years after drafting Rantanen — and again picking near the top of the draft — Sakic added a generational talent on the blue line to the mix. Cale Makar, after an extra season at UMass, arrived on the scene with "star caliber" as his baseline. He has since gone supernova. Watching him play while trying to suss out spots where he could improve is a challenge. Watching him play in any other context is a treat.

Makar looks different because he is different, and he spent one of his off nights during the Final accepting the Norris Trophy as the league's best defenseman. It was his first; it won't be his last. He capped his season by adding a Conn Smythe to his trophy case.

If you believe that to be Colorado's core, it was in place by 2018. The years after were marked by second-round playoff failures and the requisite roster work from Sakic's group. In came Devon Toews, a ready-made, top-pair running mate for Makar who cost all of two second-round draft picks. In came Nazem Kadri, who brought both elite down-the-middle depth and a dramatic arc all his own. In came Valeri Nichushkin and Artturi Lehkonen and Darcy Kuemper and more names you'll see in the following pages and, sometime soon, etched on the greatest trophy in sports.

This summer, each of these players will get their chance to carry that trophy to the beach. Or to the mountains. Or along a parade route. Or home. ▬▬

Fantastic Finnish

Rantanen, Lehkonen Shine as Avs Take Game 1 in Overtime

By Peter Baugh

JUNE 16, 2022

Midway through Mikko Rantanen's scrum at Stanley Cup Final media day, a Finnish TV analyst slid through the crowd of reporters and placed a bar of Fazer chocolate on his podium. Rantanen smiled, recognizing both the Finnish treat and the face of the person who gave it to him. It was Ismo Lehkonen, who works for the Finnish Broadcasting Company and also happens to be the father of Artturi Lehkonen, one of Rantanen's Avalanche teammates.

Artturi made sure not to miss out on the chocolate. He carried a pair of Frazer bars in the pocket of his shorts during his media scrum. It's the only unhealthy food he allows himself to snack on, according to his dad. "No chips," Ismo said from the auxiliary press seats Wednesday in Ball Arena. "The only sweets he eats is that."

What makes it different from chocolate in North America? Artturi's answer is simple, though perhaps not descriptive.

"It's just so much better. In every way," he said. "There's no doubt about it."

Beyond their shared appreciation for their homeland's chocolate, the Finnish duo of Rantanen and Lehkonen has been a boon for Colorado. They help keep the lineup balanced, with Rantanen currently carrying the second line and Lehkonen on the third. Both play on the Avalanche's top power-play unit.

In the opening night Stanley Cup Final contest, Rantanen and Lehkonen left their fingerprints all over Colorado's 4-3 win against Tampa Bay. Rantanen had two assists, including one on a perfect pass to Lehkonen waiting backdoor on a five-on-three power play. Lehkonen buried that look and also had a pair of clears playing on the Avalanche penalty kill. Each had impressive underlying numbers as well. Colorado had 91.91 percent of the five-on-five expected goal share with Rantanen on the ice and 70.57 percent with Lehkonen, according to Natural Stat Trick.

The two grew up near each other in their native country and train together with Ismo in the off-season, and Rantanen was thrilled when Colorado traded for Lehkonen in March. Now they are thriving on hockey's biggest stage.

"(Lehkonen) has always been a gamer, especially in the playoffs," Rantanen said. "He's been scoring big goals for us. He goes to the hard areas. He's not scared of anything, even though he's not the biggest guy."

Rantanen, who had the first scoring chance of the Final with a backhand shot snared by Andrei Vasilevskiy, was one of the most noticeable players in Game 1. With him on the ice, the Avalanche had seven scoring chances (only two against), three high-danger chances (zero against) and 22 shot attempts (11 against), according to Natural Stat Trick.

Ismo, who did live intermission reports broadcast in Finland, believes Rantanen has relaxed as the postseason has gone on, especially after the Avalanche made it past the second round, which had been their downfall the previous three seasons.

"He was a little bit nervous because the pressure was so high," Ismo said. "I told the Finnish people, 'Third round, he's going to be playing well. Don't worry about it. He's going to be a horse now.'"

He was right. Rantanen has four of his five playoff goals in the past five games.

Asked if the chocolate had anything to do with his success, Rantanen admitted he's not planning to have any until the offseason.

"I'll try to stay out of (it) for the next two weeks," he said. "My girlfriend ate a little bit, so maybe that was good luck."

What's it like for Ismo covering a series in which his son is playing? Well, he's transparent about his rooting interests.

"It's weird, but everybody in Finland knows this, and I tell them, 'I'm on Colorado's wagon,'" Ismo said. "Everybody understands that." ▬▬

Close to Perfect

Avalanche Reach Another Level in Game 2 Rout of Lightning

By Peter Baugh

JUNE 19, 2022

L ess than two hours before puck drop before Game 2, Tampa Bay coach Jon Cooper made his expectations clear. There wouldn't be a repeat of the first 10 minutes of Game 1, which saw Colorado score twice before the first period was half over.

"I expect us to be way the heck better," Cooper said.

One team was way the heck better than it was in Game 1, and not just in the first 10 minutes of the game. It just wasn't the Lightning.

"They're just playing at a much higher level than we are right now," Cooper said following Colorado's 7-0 bludgeoning in Game 2. "I think it was evident watching that game."

Added Colorado coach Jared Bednar, "It was certainly as close to perfect of a game as you can get from your players."

The Avalanche jumped on Tampa like a trampoline. J.T. Compher drew a penalty a minute into the contest, and though the top power-play unit couldn't generate many high-danger chances, the player of the game came through when the second unit took the ice. Valeri Nichushkin — the winger bought out three summers ago by Dallas after a goalless season — tapped in a perfectly placed pass from Andre Burakovsky. He roared with excitement as he skated toward his teammate.

"(Nichushkin) is such a hard-working guy, and it shows on ice," Avs defenseman Cale Makar said. "He's so valuable for us in every single zone. ... He's the full package."

Colorado didn't relent after Nichushkin's opening goal, as two of general manager Joe Sakic's trade deadline acquisitions teamed up for the team's second tally. Andrew Cogliano, back in the lineup after missing Game 1 with a finger injury, shoveled the puck to Josh Manson, and the two former Ducks charged forward for a two-on-one. Manson zinged it past Andrei Vasilevskiy.

"To share that one with Cogs, obviously it was nice," Manson said. "I just knew I wasn't giving it back to him."

It was yet another example of Sakic's acquisitions coming through. Manson has a goal in every round of these playoffs but the first, and he had a key shot block in Colorado's close-out Game 6 win against St. Louis. Artturi Lehkonen has seven goals, including the overtime winner against Edmonton to send Colorado to the Stanley Cup Final, and Cogliano has two game-winning tallies this postseason. Even Nico Sturm, a healthy scratch at points this postseason, assisted a Round 1 overtime winner.

"We've been lucky to fit in here with this team," Manson said. "They do such a great job making us comfortable and fitting us into their system."

Six minutes later came Burakovsky's second goal of the series. He batted in a Mikko Rantanen rebound to give Colorado a three-goal lead. Unfortunately for the Avalanche, Burakovsky left the game early in the second period after a Victor Hedman pass hit him in the hand. Bednar said the winger, who is having a standout series, will need further evaluation.

At points in earlier series, Colorado let teams get back into games after seizing large leads. The Avalanche nearly blew a 4-1 lead in Game 4 of the St. Louis second-round series, then let a 3-0 lead slip away a game later. In the next round against Edmonton, the Avalanche let the Oilers back into Game 1 after seizing a 7-3 advantage.

Those setbacks proved to be lessons for Avalanche players.

"We've been learning since the start of the playoffs, since the start of the season, really," said rookie Alex Newhook, who notched his first two finals points with a pair of assists Saturday. "We know that if we play our game and don't get away from it, it's going to be hard for any team to beat us."

Colorado carried that mindset into the second period and found success. Nichushkin scored early, then Darren Helm, who finished the game with 12 hits, added another on a breakaway.

Nichushkin would have had a hat trick had Vasilevskiy not robbed him in the second, sliding across the crease.

By period's end, Colorado held a 5-0 lead, and Lightning players looked visibly frustrated, at times losing their composure. Corey Perry, after taking a roughing minor in the first, got into a tussle with Compher in the crease and got up by pressing his knee into the Colorado forward's ankle. Ross Colton also had a knee-on-knee hit on star defenseman Makar earlier in the period. But Colorado didn't let it interrupt any focus.

"We can't think that we're under their skin," Manson said. "We can't think anything like that. We've just got to keep going."

Entering the third period, the Avalanche hadn't gotten a goal in the series from arguably their three best players: Makar, Nathan MacKinnon and Rantanen. That changed in a hurry in the third. After a Rantanen tripping penalty, Makar snatched a puck on the penalty kill, burst up ice and scored on a two-on-one with Cogliano.

"(He was) able to get a little break and get an opportunity to go the other way," Cogliano said. "And he's up the ice so fast they can't recover."

After taking a cross-check from Ondrej Palat, Makar added another goal, this time on the ensuing power play. He buried a cross-ice pass from Rantanen, who finished the game with a team-best three points, all assists.

By game's end, the numbers were jarringly in the Avalanche's favor. They led 7-1 in high-danger chances, 21-6 in scoring chances and had 82.93 percent of the expected goals share, according to Natural Stat Trick. Colorado even won the goaltending battle, with Darcy Kuemper stopping all 16 shots he faced, including a big save on Perry off a faceoff.

"He was exactly what we needed him to be," Manson said.

Colorado also dominated the special teams battle, scoring twice on the power play and another time on the penalty kill. It was just another edge in a near-perfect performance.

"I thought it was exceptional," Bednar said about the team's relentlessness. "I thought our guys played hard right from the drop of the puck. Highly committed on the defensive side of things. Dangerous offensively. We were tenacious on pucks, relentless puck pursuit. And that was throughout our entire lineup."

By the end of the game, the fans in attendance were partying more than watching, singing along to "All the Small Things" as loud as ever, as well as finishing a verse of "My Own Worst Enemy." "We want the Cup!" calls started in the first and returned periodically throughout the game, and the crowd also unleashed a "Perry sucks!" chant directed at the Lightning forward.

The Avalanche played the type of defensive game Tampa was supposed to play, smothering their opponent, forechecking hard and limiting shots. They also played the type of offensive game the Avalanche were supposed to play, making crisp passes, finishing their chances and using their speed to cause headaches for Tampa.

"I feel like we played to our identity to a T tonight," Makar said. "But at the end of the day, we know next game they're going to bring their best. It's always the next game that is the hardest."

Especially against a team like Tampa. The Lightning players are no strangers to these situations. They dropped their first two games to New York in this year's Eastern Conference final, too, before rebounding to win four in a row.

But these Avalanche are not those Rangers. This is a team with elite talent and notable depth playing at its peak, one that looks as formidable as any Tampa has seen the past three postseasons. But there's no use sitting back and letting the hunger subside, especially against a team with a championship pedigree.

"In our room we have that humble mentality and that belief," Manson said. "If we go out and play the way that we need to play, we have confidence in ourselves. We have belief in our game." ▬▬

Reality Check

Avalanche Face Questions, and Not Just in Net, After Game 3 Trouncing

By Peter Baugh

JUNE 21, 2022

Colorado can probably expect to lose the goaltending battle in the Stanley Cup Final. Most teams will when going against superstar netminder Andrei Vasilevskiy. That doesn't mean the Avalanche should lose the series — they've shown the ability to dominate Tampa Bay's skaters — but it does mean they can't afford to give away goals. And that's what happened Monday in Game 3, in equal part because of an uninspiring Darcy Kuemper outing and because of defensive breakdowns.

Kuemper left the game midway through the second period, having surrendered five goals on 22 shots faced. According to Evolving-Hockey, he had saved 2.25 fewer goals than expected. Now coach Jared Bednar faces a choice: Does he stick with Kuemper, his starter all season, or turn to No. 2 Pavel Francouz, who has six wins this postseason, including all four of Colorado's victories in the Western Conference final? Bednar didn't offer any clarity on his thought process postgame, saying the staff will go about making its decision the same way it always does.

"(Kuemper) didn't have a good night. Neither did our team," Bednar said after his team's 6-2 loss, which cut Colorado's series lead to 2-1. "We win as a team, lose as a team. I'm going to group him in with everyone else."

Since taking a stick to the face in Game 3 of the Nashville series, which forced him to miss a game, Kuemper has saved more goals than expected in only two of his 11 starts, per Evolving-Hockey. He has saved 8.16 fewer goals since the start of Round 1, the worst mark of any netminder this postseason. That's a cumulative statistic, so it's a tad misleading — Ville Husso saved 5.13 goals fewer than expected but played in only seven games — but it's still problematic for the Avalanche.

Kuemper started the game strong, robbing Ross Colton with a pad save and deflecting an ensuing Nick Paul shot off a rebound. And when the Avalanche took the lead on a Gabriel Landeskog power-play goal, they appeared in good shape.

But Tampa Bay pushed back and pushed back hard. That started with Anthony Cirelli's first goal of the series. The center cut through the neutral zone and moved the puck to Patrick Maroon, who fed it back to him. With the puck on his stick, Cirelli drove toward the net. He seemed to lose track of the puck, but that ended up working in his favor. The puck rolled off his stick and went through the legs of Kuemper, who might've missed a chance to poke away the puck as Cirelli blasted toward him.

The Avalanche's defense didn't do its netminder any favors. With just more than five minutes left in the first period, Devon Toews flubbed a pass to Cale Makar, handing Tampa Bay's top line a rush attempt. The Lightning stars delivered. Ondrej Palat got the puck to Steven Stamkos and then zipped to the slot, where his captain found him with a pass. Palat zipped a shot past Kuemper's blocker to give Tampa Bay its first lead of the series.

"Defensively, we've got some things to clean up," Landeskog said. "Our exits weren't as good, and we allowed them some quality scoring chances that we haven't done so far in the series."

Then, early in the second, Colton capitalized on a sloppy Josh Manson turnover. Colton seized the puck along the boards and found Paul, battling through an apparent lower-body injury, in the slot. The deadline acquisition capitalized.

"I went to go reverse it, thinking that was the play to be made," Manson said. "We had a couple lapses in coverage, a couple breakdowns, a couple turnovers, and they scored. ... That's why they've won two (consecutive) championships. They capitalize on their opportunities, they stay patient."

Colorado once again cut the lead to one goal with a Landeskog power-play tally, but another defensive breakdown cost the Avalanche when Nikita Kucherov found Stamkos in the slot with a slick pass. Kucherov is a Hart Trophy winner and arguably the most dynamic playmaking winger in the game. It's understandable that he'll make sharp plays. But leaving Stamkos, one of the best goal scorers of this generation, alone in the slot is asking for a goal against.

Those types of plays plagued the Avalanche throughout the first 40 minutes. According to NHL Network's Mike Kelly, who specializes in analytics, Tampa Bay had 10 inner-slot shots in the first two periods, compared to only three for Colorado.

"We gave up too many slot chances that we didn't give up in the first two games," Mikko Rantanen said. "It's just about finding the guy behind you. They're a very good team. They're going to get behind you if you don't take a look."

Kuemper finally got the hook after allowing a goal to Maroon. The winger, who had just left the penalty box after offsetting roughing minors with Manson, zipped toward the net with the puck. As he neared the crease, he backhanded the puck up Kuemper's arm and into the net.

"He's been great all year," Nathan MacKinnon said of Kuemper. "I'm not going to get down on him at all. ... Tough bounces for him, too."

Francouz held his own in relief, saving nine of 10 shots faced. The one goal he allowed came off the stick of Corey Perry, who batted in an already tipped Victor Hedman shot that sneaked into the crease.

Though Kuemper struggled, Vasilevskiy was masterful. He twice robbed J.T. Compher from potting rebound attempts by getting his skate across the crease to block the puck and finished with 37 saves.

"He looks like himself," MacKinnon said. "He's been the best in the league for four or five years now, so I'm not surprised."

For the Avalanche, making a goalie change would be a risk, and it feels unlikely. If Bednar makes a switch, he could thwart Kuemper's confidence, and that could come back to bite the Avalanche if Francouz struggles. Perhaps the wisest move would be to stick with Kuemper, then switch netminders if he shows any sign of trouble early in Game 4.

"We know Kuemps is a great goalie," Rantanen said. "He's going to bounce back like everybody else."

The Finnish winger said the locker room wasn't quiet postgame. The Avalanche know it's not easy to win three in a row against Tampa Bay, and they know they have to move on. And assuming Kuemper keeps the starter's net, he'll have to be part of that effort.

"It's just about learning and moving on right away," Rantanen said. "We've got to just look at it tomorrow a little bit, what we can do better. Clean up a couple mistakes and go at it again." ■■■

'Can't Make That Stuff Up'

Inside Nazem Kadri's Avalanche Return and an OT Cup Final Goal for the Ages

By Peter Baugh

JUNE 23, 2022

Nazem Kadri and the postseason, for good or for bad, will always go together. He knows his reputation will always carry three playoff suspensions, two with Toronto and one with Colorado, all three of which might have prevented his team from advancing. But now there's more to Kadri's postseason legacy than the painful, costly moments. There's glory, resilience and, as of Wednesday night, one of the biggest goals in Colorado Avalanche history.

Thumb surgery earlier this month put Kadri's postseason — and the rest of his Avalanche tenure, given his status as a pending unrestricted free agent — in question. But the center worked his way back and, with the Avalanche looking to take a 3-1 series lead in the Stanley Cup Final, received an overtime pass from Artturi Lehkonen entering the offensive zone. He darted forward, shifted to his left, past Mikhail Sergachev, and wristed the puck into the top of the net.

With that, the Avalanche had a 3-2 win, bringing them within one win of hockey's ultimate prize.

"It's an inspiration to everybody else to see a teammate like that try to come back and fight

every day to try to get better," captain Gabriel Landeskog said of Kadri. "You can't make that stuff up."

It's the type of play you remember for life. Every detail.

Everyone froze, but the youngest player on the ice knew Kadri had scored. Bowen Byram, who'd hit the crossbar with a shot earlier in overtime, saw the top of the net flex as puck hit twine, and he sprinted through the neutral zone, right toward the official, pointing excitedly. He was right. It was a goal.

One No. 91 collided with another. Edmonton was a minute into hosting its first Western Conference final game since 2006 when winger Evander Kane, still this postseason's leader in goals, used his stick to force Kadri headfirst into the boards.

Kadri went down hard. He didn't get up. His thumb was hurt, and he thought he was done.

"Roller coaster of emotions, thinking I was done, then having a sliver of hope," he said after his Game 4 goal. "Sitting here right now is kind of surreal."

Landeskog had just sat down on the bench, legs tired, when he looked up and saw Kadri on a partial breakaway. Then the puck disappeared. Some Avalanche players on the bench, including Logan O'Connor, were confident Kadri had scored. But Landeskog waited, not wanting to celebrate until he saw the puck. When he did, he rushed onto the ice, helping pin Kadri against the glass. Their heads bounced together in celebration.

Two days after the Kane hit, TSN posted a report of Kadri's surgery on Instagram, saying he was unlikely to return before the end of the postseason. The Avalanche center saw the post and, always confident, left a comment.

"Ya we'll see.."

After the June 6 surgery, the sense was that the team would be able to evaluate a potential Kadri return two weeks post-operation. Until then, he skated with skills coach Shawn Allard, adding a stick to his routine last week.

Kadri got closer and closer, and on Tuesday, the day before Game 4, took the ice with his teammates for an optional practice.

"Naz is a big-time player for us," teammate Mikko Rantanen said. "It's nice to see him back on the ice and working again."

Vasilevskiy, the greatest goalie of his generation, didn't argue. He turned around and watched, eyes wide, as Tampa Bay captain Steven Stamkos dislodged the puck. The netminder stood slowly, skated off the ice, and then walked out of the arena, an undone light blue tie around his neck.

Avalanche coach Jared Bednar wanted to talk to Kadri. He didn't just want to hear the trainers say the center was ready.

"I wanted to know what he's able to do, what he can't do, if anything, how he's feeling about it, making sure that he's confident he can come back and help," the coach said. "I don't want him in if he can't play the right way and accomplish what we need to accomplish. He was pretty sure, liked how his skates have gone. So, obviously we want a player of his caliber in the lineup."

Kadri said he had a good sense Tuesday that he'd play, then the team reached an official decision Wednesday morning.

Ismo Lehkonen, whose son, Artturi, assisted the goal, watched on a TV monitor from the Amalie Arena media room. A broadcaster for Finnish television, he was in Tampa for the game, and he "wondered what the heck people were doing." When Ismo realized Kadri had scored, he viewed it as a reward. Artturi and Kadri, the primary assister on the goal and scorer, had both worked hard all game. They stuck with their process, even after getting outplayed in the first period and even when posts and Vasilevskiy robbed the Avalanche of a win earlier in the overtime period.

"Just keep working," said Ismo, who was a longtime Finnish coach. "Trust your system. Trust your skating. Trust every part of it."

Kadri was one of the last Avalanche players to join pregame warm-ups, and he tried out a light shot almost immediately after taking the ice. He deflected questions about his ability to shoot and how healthy he was, saying only that he felt "good enough."

But he clearly wasn't 100 percent, battling the ice — which he called "kind of garbage" during an ESPN interview at first intermission — and at times the puck, especially in the first period. He looked tentative, both with his shot and going into the boards.

At game's end, though, he had played nearly 19 minutes, and the Avalanche had 77 percent of the expected goals when he was on the ice, according to Natural Stat Trick.

"I thought it was good, start to finish," Bednar said.

Watching from Denver, Ashley Kadri, Nazem's wife, thought Vasilevskiy had the puck tucked under his arm. And in London, Ontario, where Nazem grew up, his close friend Jason McNeil ran around his living room until his TV showed the puck was in the net. "Then nearly jumped through the floor," he said. He immediately booked flights to Denver for Game 5.

It feels almost fitting that Kadri's biggest postseason moment came with a dash of controversy. After the game, Lightning coach Jon Cooper abruptly left midway through his first answer, too upset to speak. He implied Kadri's goal shouldn't have counted.

After Cooper's comments, it became clear that Tampa Bay felt there were too many men on the ice. The league's hockey operations department put out a statement shortly after, saying "each of the four officials advised that they did not see a too-many-men-on-the-ice situation on the play."

"I'm not quite sure what he's thinking, why it shouldn't have counted," Kadri said. "That kind of confuses me a little bit. The puck hit the back of the net."

And that's what mattered for the Avalanche.

"End of story," he said.

Kadri thought the puck was in. Then he didn't. He had tried to go far side, and he knew he'd gotten a good shot off. But judging by Vasilevskiy's reaction in the crease, he thought the goalie had pinned the puck between his arm and body. The confusion ended when he saw his teammates rush toward him. He'd worked for moments like these.

"This," he said, "is what I've been waiting for my whole life." ▬▬

Celebration Delayed

Confidence Still High After Avalanche Miss Chance to Clinch in 'Even-Played' Game 5

By Peter Baugh

JUNE 25, 2022

With the Avalanche down a goal late in the third period of Game 5, Nathan MacKinnon jumped onto the ice. He wanted to make something happen, wanted the Avalanche to complete a comeback and clinch the Stanley Cup in front of their home fans. So when the star center received a pass, he blazed up ice and put a shot on Lightning goaltender Andrei Vasilevskiy.

Unfortunately for MacKinnon and the Avalanche, he had left the bench too soon, jumping into play while J.T. Compher was skating across the team logo at center ice. The officials blew the play dead and called a bench minor. Too many men.

"We left early," coach Jared Bednar conceded after his team's 3-2 loss in Game 5. "The puck kind of popped out to center ice, guys were on their way to the bench. We left early."

In a game in which the Avalanche seemed to have multiple gripes with officiating, this wasn't one worth debating. It was a cut-and-dried call, and it cost Colorado a chance to pull goaltender Darcy Kuemper before the final 40 seconds of regulation.

The penalty also came with some irony. Two nights before, Lightning coach Jon Cooper had lamented Nazem Kadri's Game 4 overtime winner, implying that Colorado had too many men on the ice for the goal.

"(The Game 4 comments) shouldn't be a story," Cooper said after the game. "The refs called the game by the rules. It was fortunate for us because instead of them having a three-minute goalie pull, they only get 40 seconds."

And those 40 seconds weren't enough for Bednar's team to beat Vasilevskiy. When the final horn sounded, Colorado led in shots (37-29) and five-on-five scoring chances (25-18, per Natural Stat Trick). But Colorado trailed in five-on-five high-danger chances (7-6), and Vasilevskiy — Tampa Bay's ultimate trump card — proved hard to beat, even if Bednar liked the chances Colorado got on Tampa's net. "I didn't mind them," he said. "We were getting to the net, there were a bunch of scrambles again, some good looks. (Vasilevskiy) made some big saves, as did Kuemps. A pretty even-played game all the way through."

The Avalanche were frequenting the box early in the game, which Bednar believes gave the Lightning's top players some momentum. Compher committed a high-sticking infraction minutes into the first period, and Kadri followed with a hooking penalty. The Avalanche's penalty kill stood strong, though, and Colorado even had a chance to take the lead after MacKinnon drew a trip midway through the period. But with the packed Ball Arena crowd buzzing, the home team couldn't capitalize.

With about five minutes left in the period, Tampa Bay's Jan Rutta skated into the offensive zone and unleashed a slap shot on net. It whizzed past Kuemper's glove to give the Lightning the lead. It was one Bednar would have liked to see his goaltender snag, though he added that he liked Kuemper's battle throughout the contest.

"It was a little bit of a knuckler," said Kuemper, who stopped 26 shots. "You know, you do things the right way. That's all you can do. Obviously, you don't want to let any goals in. But it happens."

Colorado pushed after the goal. MacKinnon nearly scored on a breakaway set up by Devon Toews, trying to poke a puck through Vasilevskiy's legs, but the puck went just wide. Gabriel Landeskog had an open look shortly after, but the Tampa Bay netminder stymied him. Early in the second period, though, the Avalanche broke through. Vasilevskiy couldn't grab a shot off the stick of Cale Makar, who was as dynamic as ever, and Valeri Nichushkin burst in to clean up the rebound in the crease and tie the score.

"He's been good all season long, all playoffs," Bednar said of the Russian winger. "This is no different. He's a beast for us."

The officials called offsetting penalties on Compher and Alex Killorn, then Makar got called for hooking, handing the Lightning a four-on-three advantage. Though Bednar and Landeskog tried not to critique the officiating too openly, they made it clear afterward that they didn't like the penalty on Makar.

"I didn't love that call, just because there was no intent there," Bednar said. "I don't even think he was checking that guy. Looked to me like he kind of tripped over a stick. It's a tough one."

"Some of those calls we probably could've done without," Landeskog said. "But at the end of the day, we're trying to focus on what we've got to do."

During Tampa Bay's four-on-three, Colorado's unit of Josh Manson, Darren Helm and Jack Johnson tried to shut down shooting lanes but couldn't find a way to gain possession and clear the puck. And against a star-studded Lightning group, that proved costly. Nikita Kucherov ripped a shot off the post and in for his first goal of the series. With that, Tampa Bay reclaimed the lead.

Colorado drew a penalty late in the second when Ross Colton high-sticked Logan O'Connor, and the Avalanche thought they should have gotten a five-on-three after a Nick Paul clear attempt went over the glass. The officials ruled it hit the boards, though, and a fan threw a beer can on the ice in disgust.

During the power play, Makar darted toward the net and split two defenders. Both hit the Avalanche star on his hands with their sticks, and the normally mild-mannered defenseman called angrily for a penalty.

But Makar would be contained for only so long. Early in the third, he fired a shot from the offensive zone faceoff circle, and Vasilevskiy allowed a rebound that went off Erik Cernak's skate and past the netminder. Tampa Bay didn't fold, though, and Makar found himself on the wrong end of a goal with less than seven minutes left. Ondrej Palat escaped the star defenseman and netted a winning one-timer from the slot, and the Avalanche couldn't find a way to equalize the score one final time. The series moved back to Tampa for Game 6.

"I lose an assignment on the goal," said Makar, who finished with a goal and assist and drove play throughout the game. "Can't happen."

Bednar said he wouldn't put Palat's goal all on Makar, noting that "a little bit of communication there probably solves that."

The Avalanche have two remaining chances to win one game and capture the Stanley Cup. Although Game 5 came with disappointment, Colorado players expressed confidence that they could get the job done.

"We won (in Tampa) last time (in Game 4), so we've just gotta go out there and play our game and stay even-keel through the highs and the lows," Kuemper said. "We would have taken a 3-2 series lead any day. We're in a good spot here."

Said Landeskog: "We'll wake up tomorrow, we'll be ready to go, watch some film and see where we can get better and see where we can tighten things up to make it harder for them.

"We'll bounce right back." ■■■■

'All These Champions Skating Around'

Inside the Avalanche's Cup celebration

By Peter Baugh

JUNE 27, 2022

Standing on the ice at Amalie Arena, soaking in sweat and tears and the emotions that come with reaching hockey's peak, Gabriel Landeskog harkened back to his draft day, back to when he was clean-shaven and had a full career ahead of him. He told reporters at the time that he had a photo of Peter Forsberg and the 2001 Avalanche Stanley Cup team hanging from his bedroom wall in Stockholm. His goal — his dream — was to be in a picture like that one day.

He finally got his wish.

After Colorado's 2-1 victory in Game 6 of the Stanley Cup Final, Landeskog looked around him, surveying his jubilant teammates.

"I'm just so happy to see all these champions skating around," he said.

As captain, Landeskog was the first to hoist the Stanley Cup. And as much as he'd longed to touch the trophy, he couldn't wait to give it away. He'd made a promise during harder times — before Cale Makar and Presidents' Trophy contention — to teammate Erik Johnson, his close friend and the longest-tenured Avalanche player. Be ready, he had said. Because whatever day the Avalanche won the Stanley Cup, he'd hand Johnson the trophy first.

"If that doesn't give you motivation, I don't know what does," Johnson said. "Who would've thought? Five years ago, dead last in the NHL. Now we're Stanley Cup champions."

As the final horn sounded, Johnson and Nathan MacKinnon met, tackling each other away from the rest of the main group. They rolled around, embracing one another. Both were on the 2016-17 team that had one of the worst seasons of the NHL's salary-cap era, logging only 48 points in the standings — more than 20 worse than the next-closest team. And in the post-win celebration, the remaining players from that roster — Landeskog, Johnson, MacKinnon, Mikko Rantanen and J.T. Compher — gathered for a picture near center ice, finally as victorious as could be.

"It's special no matter how you win this thing," Compher said. "But in the few years since that season, seeing all the work that's gone in..."

MacKinnon, who scored the game-tying goal in the second period, found his parents, Graham and Kathy, as soon as they walked onto the ice. He cried in his dad's arms. "I kind of get flashbacks to my whole childhood, my whole life," said the center, who finished second to Makar in Conn Smythe Trophy voting. "It feels amazing."

Makar, the defenseman who moves the puck like a yo-yo and skates like a gazelle, completed a rare combo with the Norris Trophy and Conn Smythe this season. And he had help: His mom, Laura, had ditched her lucky outfit after the Avalanche's Game 5 loss, and she ate kale salads ahead of games 4 and 6, both Colorado victories. A mother's touch works wonders.

Laura wasn't alone in attendance. Cale's dad, Gary, was there, too, as well as Taylor, Cale's younger brother and a 2021 Avalanche seventh-round draft pick.

"Growing up, playing mini-sticks when we were little kids, getting in fights, stuff like that," Taylor said. "It's everything he's always wanted, what our family has wanted."

Around the ice, players FaceTimed with loved ones who couldn't make the trip. Andre Burakovsky shared a moment on the phone with his dad, Robert, and Bowen Byram grinned into a screen at his sister, Jamie. "I'll drink your share of the beer," their dad, Shawn, joked.

Johnson accidentally knocked Sportsnet contributor Ken Wiebe's recorder out of his hands while reaching for a family member's phone. He apologized as Wiebe jokingly called for a two-minute roughing penalty.

Darren Helm cried while holding his daughter. Makar stood arm-in-arm with Devon Toews, his defensive partner. Andrew Cogliano's mom pulled Jack Johnson in for a hug. Erik Johnson said he needed a beer. (And there was plenty to come later in the evening.)

There was Nazem Kadri, his thumb still bandaged. He broke it in multiple places but found a way to turn a six-week recovery into two. Burakovsky battled through a broken ankle to play the first two Stanley Cup Final games but was finally kept out by a thumb injury. Cogliano, who has played 1,140 regular-season games, waiting and hoping for this moment, played with pins in his broken middle finger. Worth it?

"Fuckin' right," he said.

To reach their goal, the Avalanche had to knock off the two-time-defending Cup champion Lightning. And after taking the lead in the second period, Colorado executed a clinical third, limiting Tampa Bay to only two shots on goal and generating a plethora of scoring chances the other way. With a clear at the final horn, the game ended. The Avalanche had won.

"We went out there and probably played one of the most perfect clinching third periods in the history of hockey," Byram said.

Added goalie Darcy Kuemper, who finished the night with 22 saves: "That was some of the best hockey I've ever watched. To have the Cup on the line and come out like we did and not give up everything, it was a special effort."

General manager Joe Sakic, the team's architect, posed for pictures with his family, and he said hello to Toews' parents, Werner and Tammy, who thanked him for taking on a chance on their son in a 2020 trade from the New York Islanders. It's a deal Sakic would do a million times over: He paid only two second-round picks for Toews, and the defenseman has finished 11th and eighth in Norris Trophy voting the past two years, respectively.

"I don't know if it's really soaked in yet," Werner said. "It's incredible. It's a hard road."

A little before 2 a.m. Eastern, the Cup left the building in the hands of a jubilant Landeskog, whose mood was perhaps buoyed by a couple of drinks. A procession of teammates walked with him, including Josh Manson with an NHL championship belt over his shoulder, and Makar with Oakley goggles — champagne protection — on his forehead. "Post that on Twitter!" Byram yelled,

wearing an unbuttoned shirt and suit jacket while double-fisting champagne bottles. Landeskog showed off the trophy to the media members still at the rink working, with one message to share.

"We're taking it back to Denver!"

Valeri Nichushkin and MacKinnon were among the last to leave. Nichushkin, dealing with a suspected foot injury, got a ride from a stadium worker on a flatbed dolly usually used for transporting crates, a bottle in his left hand. MacKinnon walked behind him, laughing at his teammate, victorious at last. ▄▄

ROAD TO

THE CUP

Cale Makar

Diss Tracks, Dorm Life and a 2-Year Plan
to Build an Avalanche Star

By Peter Baugh

FEBRUARY 21, 2022

Before Greg Carvel could change the program, he needed to keep the program-changer. And that meant he had a clear top priority when UMass hired him as men's hockey coach in March 2016: Call Cale Makar.

Makar, a young defenseman from Calgary who had committed to the previous coaching staff, was getting a flurry of interest from other major programs that spring. So immediately upon taking the job, Carvel started working the phones, trying to convince Makar and his family that the Minutemen remained the right fit.

It helped that Carvel, a former Ducks and Senators assistant, had experience with NHL teams. For a young player with big aspirations — and for his family — that is a draw. Ultimately, Carvel was able to make his case, and Makar reaffirmed his commitment. He was headed to Amherst, Mass.

But first, Carvel was headed to Brooks, Alberta, to meet Makar in person, making the trip up that September to watch him play with the Bandits, an Alberta league junior team. As he watched Makar take the ice, Carvel could see that the lofty reports that had made the young man his top priority didn't do the player justice. This rosy-cheeked youngster reminded him of a special defenseman he'd coached in Ottawa a half-decade earlier, so much so that he called one of his assistants before the first period was over.

"We have Erik Karlsson coming to our program," Carvel remembers telling him.

Makar's decision to stick with UMass not only shaped the program's future but also his own. In 2017, he arrived on campus as a notable prospect — the Avalanche had selected him at No. 4 earlier that summer — but also one who needed to mature physically. Over the next two years, he built lasting friendships and impressed UMass staffers academically and athletically. By the end of his college career, he was a no-doubt NHL player.

"It was a stepping stone in my life that I'll never forget," he says.

With Makar returning to Massachusetts this week to take on the Bruins — and fresh off a 5-3 win Saturday in Buffalo, the site of his final college games — let's take a look back at that step-ping stone, and how it helped shape a person and player who hit the NHL like a lightning bolt and has progressed into a superstar in the midst of a generational season.

Diss tracks and prank battles

If you were to ask the 2017-18 UMass team which of their teammates would be most likely to write a diss track, Makar would not have been anyone's answer. He's reserved — friendly, but someone who goes about his business quietly.

But, as he's shown on the ice, he's full of surprises. In the days leading up to UMass hockey's annual freshman talent show, Makar called his dad, Gary, brainstorming good-natured lyrics to rib coaches and teammates. One line, for example, joked about a teammate hating when others touched his shoes.

"I figured I'd do something to surprise everybody," he says.

Forwards Mitchell Chaffee and Oliver Chau, two of Makar's suitemates and best friends, found out about his plan a couple days ahead of time, and Chau was a little nervous as Makar took the stage. But the reception was exactly what Makar wanted. His teammates were both shocked and amused.

"He could walk that fine line between being funny without being disrespectful," Carvel says.

Away from the rink, Makar also enjoyed cribbage matches with forward Jake Gaudet, and he called his parents every night at 10 p.m. He didn't have a game system, but he played in his friends' rooms, struggling mightily at Fortnite. Colin Felix, a freshman during Makar's sophomore year, engaged with him in prank battles. Felix once sneaked into his older teammate's room and flipped everything over, from his bed to his chair to the stuff on his desk. Makar got Felix back by wrapping everything in his room in plastic, including his dresser and TV.

"I swear I was finding things in my room wrapped up for a couple days," says Felix.

And, like most college kids, Makar loved to eat. He particularly liked the stir fry at Berkshire Dining Hall — a tasty way to eat lots of vegetables.

He quickly was on a first-name basis with the chef and liked the food spicy, Chau remembers, meaning his cheeks grew even rosier as he ate.

Winter breaks provided plenty of free time, and that's how, during Makar's sophomore year, he found himself in a band. Chau and Gaudet are competent guitar players and, while bored one day, started messing around in a room with Makar and Chaffee. With the largest social media following of the group, Makar sent out an Instagram story asking for band name submissions. That led to the suggestion "Fleetwood Mask," which the foursome adopted for their apartment jam sessions.

Makar's largest contribution to the band was his Instagram question. The rest of his role was unclear and didn't involve much music. He was either band manager, Chaffee's backup vocalist or a drummer using pots and pans, depending on who you ask.

"No performances, no albums," Chaffee jokes. "We kind of laid low."

But they had fun in the apartment, playing a mix of 2000s throwbacks, Queen and "Riptide" by Vance Joy. Chau even taught Makar some guitar.

Makar also had one last rap in him before leaving UMass. After leading the team to a Regional Championship, he brought a piece of paper into one of his teammates' rooms in the nights before they left for the NCAA semifinal. Mario Ferraro, then a fellow sophomore, remembers everyone going quiet, allowing Makar to hear a soft beat in the background. He performed yet another roast as his friends laughed.

"He's got some chirps he likes to throw in there, but it's all fun and games," Ferraro says.

As they left for the Frozen Four shortly after, Gaudet noticed Makar had packed an extra bag. Nothing was spoken, but by then it was clear: His time at UMass was coming to a close.

———————— ————————

'You'd think he was a normal student'

No one would have held it against Makar if he hadn't shown up to Richard Halgin's office. He met with the psychology professor every Wednesday morning his sophomore year for an independent reading course, but in mid-February, a snowstorm clobbered Amherst, and the university announced it would open late.

Still, at 7:50 a.m. — 10 minutes early — Halgin heard a knock.

"Cale, how did you get here?" he remembers asking as he opened the door.

"I walked," Makar responded simply, donning a maroon and gray UMass beanie. A snow-filled mile-plus trek wasn't going to keep him from an appointment.

Since he came to UMass in 1977, Halgin has taught approximately 20,000 students, including 30 PhD candidates. He says Makar is among the top five relationships he's had, and not because of hockey.

"One of the most remarkable people I've ever had the privilege of teaching," says Halgin, who now teaches Makar's brother, Taylor, a freshman on the UMass team and Avalanche draft pick. "Just the sentiment and courtesy and responsibility."

Halgin is a clinical psychologist, and for nearly three decades, he has met individually with UMass hockey players to discuss their lives. Makar saw him periodically during his freshman year and also took his abnormal psychology class. He never came late, Halgin remembers, and Chau was always impressed by the amount of notes he took.

"You wouldn't know he was a fourth overall pick," Chau says. "You'd think he was a normal student."

After Makar's freshman year, he approached Halgin about taking an independent reading course on leadership. Using recommendations from his dad, he put together a syllabus of six books for the semester, written by a range of authors, from Angela Duckworth to Simon Sinek. He proceeded to write a critical analysis off each book and, rather than using a Kindle or eReader, brought physical copies of the texts to each Wednesday meeting. The professor noticed how thoroughly Makar highlighted the pages.

"If any student had done this, I would've said, 'This guy is serious,'" Halgin says. "Cale's not going for his PhD in psychology. He's taking this as seriously as the students who are."

At the end of the term, Makar turned in a lengthy paper comparing the themes of the books with current psychological research. And he wanted to keep learning, signing up for another personalized course with Halgin, this one on self-understanding. Even after he turned pro in April, Makar completed his classes and, now that he's settled in the NHL, he's talked with Halgin about chipping away at the rest of his degree.

"He just has an incredible capacity for focus," Halgin says. "It's beyond the ice. It's in his everyday life."

The Frozen Four, the Hobey and the NHL

A few weeks after Makar arrived on campus, Chau came to Halgin's office for a chat. He had played a season of junior hockey with Makar in Brooks, and the defenseman came up in conversation.

"I feel so privileged to play with the best player of my generation," Halgin remembers Chau telling him.

The proclamation felt a little grandiose to the professor at the time. Makar was a teenager who had never played a college game. Looking back, though, Chau's words were closer to the truth than Halgin could've imagined.

In 2016-17, the year before Makar arrived, the Minutemen posted a putrid 5-29-2 record, losing their final 17 games. But the next season, Carvel brought in a top-notch recruiting class featuring Makar and Ferraro, now an alternate captain with the Sharks. John Leonard, who has played NHL games, was also in that class, as was Chaffee, now a productive AHLer for the Wild.

Clearly, the talent was there to turn the program around. It turned out the buy-in to Carvel's culture of discipline and hard work was, too.

"We were starting at the bottom of the barrel," Leonard says. "We knew there was only one way, and that was up."

On one of Makar's first days on campus, he met with Carvel in his office. The coach told him they should approach his college career with a two-year plan: If he was ready to jump after freshman year, he could, but he'd probably need two before he was physically ready.

Makar was on board with the plan. He went about his business, making sure not to carry himself with arrogance, despite his pro future.

"There's a lot of stigmas that (a top draft pick) could be cocky," Chaffee says. "But he was really one of the most humble guys I've ever met."

"Such a gentleness about him," Halgin adds. "He was sort of the opposite of the stereotypes of what a professional hockey player would be."

Throughout his two seasons in Amherst, Makar showed a fierce loyalty to his school, passing up potential life-altering opportunities in order to remain. That started early. Carvel remembers spotting representatives from Hockey Canada at the first game of Makar's freshman year.

Jesus, the coach thought. They're already here to steal Cale, and he hasn't even played a game yet.

With NHLers not going to the Olympics, Hockey Canada wanted Makar to join the roster as a power-play specialist. But Makar was already planning to play for Canada at the world juniors. Adding the Olympics would have meant too much time away from school, and he probably would've had to go pro immediately after. It didn't feel right. He said no.

The day Canada won bronze, Makar was in Amherst, playing against Providence College.

"If I was going to go play in the Olympics, I would be utilized for my strengths and not be able to work on my weaknesses like I would in college, being able to play in all situations," Makar says.

Adds Carvel: "It was the first example of him showing that he really understood what was best for his development."

Makar showed promise his freshman year, but he didn't feel ready for the next level at season's end, even with the Avalanche trying to get him to Denver. Physically, he was one of the weakest Minutemen players when he arrived in Amherst, Carvel says, and his stamina wasn't what it needed to be. Carvel remembers nights he couldn't play Makar the minutes he wanted because the defenseman was out of gas.

"He was wise enough to know, 'I can't go play in the NHL if I can't get through back-to-back games at the Division I level,'" Carvel says. "I'm glad he wasn't close enough — that it wasn't a hard decision."

Makar made strides in the weight room as a sophomore, and he used his speed to create an abundance of offensive chances. Carvel had never seen a defenseman create so many breakaways.

As an alternate captain that season, Makar also took on more leadership responsibility, often turning to Halgin for advice. He was still only a sophomore, after all, and wanted to help without condescending. His thoughtful leadership approach worked. Marc Del Gaizo, who is a year younger, says Makar made him feel comfortable instantly, and his hunger for improvement stood out.

"He always looks for more," Del Gaizo says. "That's kind of his leadership style."

Once, Halgin remembers, Makar told him he yelled at a new freshman for messing up a play. But as soon as he got back to the locker room, he found the newcomer and apologized. He knew what it was like to be a beginner.

"Can you imagine?" Halgin says. "It wasn't anything harsh or terrible, but he said, 'I felt terrible.'"

By this point, Makar's stature around campus had grown. Average attendance went up more than 2,000 fans per game from the season before his arrival to his sophomore year, and Halgin remembers how excited one of his colleagues was when he met the young standout. Once, Chaffee says, a student approached Makar in the dining hall with a napkin, asking for an autograph.

This was no longer a promising player with NHL potential. This was one of the best college players in the country — a can't-miss pro.

By February 2019, Carvel was comfortable enough to say it would be best for Makar to join the Avalanche. "He needs to move on," he told The Athletic's Ryan S. Clark. Avalanche general manager Joe Sakic made trips to Amherst to watch him play, and the organization was in frequent contact about his development.

Makar would shut down conversations about his likely departure, Del Gaizo remembers. Makar believes the busy nature of his schedule helped, too. He didn't have a ton of time to think about what was coming. Still, he told Carvel the weekend before the Frozen Four that he planned to sign when the team's run ended.

"We'd gotten to the end of the line," Carvel says.

Makar had a first-period assist and was on the ice for Del Gaizo's game-winning goal in the national semifinals. The next day, he won the Hobey Baker Award. After that, though, the magic ran out. An experienced Minnesota-Duluth team outplayed UMass to win the championship game 3-0.

Talking to reporters after the loss, Makar still wore his sweat-soaked jersey. He wasn't quite ready to pull the sweater over his head, wasn't quite ready to accept he was moving on. So he sat at the table, answering questions as he clung to his final moments as a college player.

"He knew that was the last time he was going to wear it," Chau says.

Disappointment radiated from him as he spoke, but there was pride in his voice. "This program is no longer an embarrassment," he said. "Everybody can look at us as a program that's going to be successful for years."

Two years later, Makar watched from Anaheim as UMass beat St. Cloud State to win the national title. He had chills seeing his teammates' joy.

"He helped us get there," Chau says. "Obviously he didn't get to win, but he knows he was a part of it."

When Chau looked at his phone after the game, he saw a missed FaceTime from his old suitemate. He dialed him back, passing the phone around from teammate to teammate so Makar could say congratulations — so he could revel in their achievement, too.

'Just a different sweater'

In April 2019, shortly after returning to their Buffalo hotel, the defeated UMass players got a group text from their superstar teammate. Makar was in the conference room, and he asked them to join. He was about to sign with the Avalanche. It was time for goodbyes.

The Minutemen players gathered around a small circular table where Makar sat in a suit jacket. He scrawled his name on the papers in front of him and posed for a group picture.

"I think it was really good to soften the moment of loss," Gary Makar says.

The next morning, he was on a flight to Denver, where the Avalanche were preparing for Game 3 of the first round against Calgary, his hometown team.

"When you (talked) to him in the meetings for the preparation, he didn't seem overwhelmed at all," Avalanche coach Jared Bednar says. "He gave you a quiet sense of confidence that he'd be able to come in and help us."

On April 15, 2019, less than 48 hours removed from the NCAA championship game, the coaching staff told him he'd be in the lineup. Makar barely had time to think, and that proved beneficial.

"It was just hockey," he says. "Just a different sweater."

Back in Amherst, Gaudet watched from an off-campus house where many UMass players live. Chaffee was there, too, and had a feeling Makar would find a way to score. At North Apartments, Del Gaizo had the same sense. He looks freaking awesome, he remembers thinking.

Sure enough, with four minutes left in the first period, Makar trailed Nathan MacKinnon into the offensive zone. MacKinnon dropped the puck to his new teammate and, skating through the slot, Makar wristed a shot past goaltender Mike Smith. Full of adrenaline, he punched the air, and captain Gabriel Landeskog wrapped him in a hug.

Gary and Laura, Makar's parents, were in the stands for the goal, having arrived in Denver just in time for puck drop. The NBC cameras focused on Gary, who sported a shocked grin as he took a photo of the Jumbotron, his phone case featuring a UMass cardholder.

"You can't write that stuff," Gary says. "Somebody sprinkled magic lucky dust on you."

After the game, Gary and Laura were in the bowels of the arena, waiting in the family lounge for their son, when MacKinnon and Landeskog approached to introduce themselves. A little starstruck, Gary asked for a photo. As he smiled for the camera with two stars, Cale walked around the corner, and Gary remembers his face turning white with embarrassment.

"It was like 'Oh my God, my dad, the biggest nerd on the planet, is taking a picture with MacKinnon and Landeskog,'" Gary says.

Colorado would ultimately beat Calgary in five games, then lose a seven-game, second-round series with San Jose. But all that mattered that night was Makar's arrival. It was a time of adrenaline, excitement and hope for the newcomer.

Naturally, the defenseman didn't let it get to his head.

The day after Makar's debut, Halgin received an email while sitting in his office. His student-turned-superstar had an earnest question: He knew he had a paper due the next morning for his independent reading course, but would it be possible to get an extension? He'd had a busy few days. ▬▬▬

Walk the (Blue) Line

Cale Makar's Skating Has the Hockey World in Awe

By Peter Baugh

FEBRUARY 22, 2022

L ofty comparisons aren't anything new when it comes to Avalanche defenseman Cale Makar, whether it's a teammate screaming that he looks like Bobby Orr after a highlight-reel goal or his coach saying he skates like Paul Coffey.

But when the greatest hockey player ever is the one making the comparison, it adds a bit of weight. So after Wayne Gretzky said before a nationally televised game that Makar reminds him of Coffey — Gretzky's former teammate, a Hall of Famer, a four-time Cup champion, a three-time Norris Trophy winner and the second-highest-scoring defenseman in NHL history — The Athletic decided to seek out Coffey himself to ask what he thinks of having his name thrown around with a 23-year-old's.

Too soon?

Quite the contrary.

"It's a compliment," Coffey says.

When Coffey watches Makar, which he does regularly, he sees a player who would have dominated any era.

"He walks the blue line as well as anyone I've ever seen," says Coffey, who himself is generally regarded as one of the best skaters ever.

Other defensive greats — from Nicklas Lidstrom to Ray Bourque to Chris Pronger — have taken notice, as well, and it's hard not to. After winning the Calder Trophy in 2019-20 and finishing second in Norris voting for 2020-21, Makar has taken another leap in his third full NHL season. The deeper you look at what he's doing, the more you see it: Makar might be more than an All-Star defenseman and a Norris contender. He might be generational.

But how is he doing it?

It all starts with his skating abilities, on display at the NHL's 2022 All-Star Game festivities. Though he didn't win the fastest skater contest, Makar was the only defenseman to participate, and his stride and smoothness were again on display as he had a pair of assists in the three-on-three game.

And with Makar, it goes beyond pure speed. Coffey, top skating coaches and other top modern skaters point to Makar's agility, sturdiness and creativity — his explosiveness off both the outside and inside edges of his skate blades — as what makes him special.

It also makes him difficult to play against. Just ask Dylan Larkin, the fastest skater competition's all-time record holder.

"You have no idea what he's going to do: It could be a hip swivel and he's down the boards and past you, or he can tiptoe across the blue line and hang onto it and then protect it or shoot it," the Red Wings forward says. "It's quite the headache."

Fun to watch, he says, but not fun to defend.

On a nightly basis, you'll see something like the highlight that went viral from an early January game against Chicago. With the score tied 3-3 in overtime, Makar skated behind the net and up the glass toward the blue line. Defended by Chicago forward Kirby Dach, he stopped on a dime and swirled toward the net. Dach bit hard, giving Makar more than the step he needed. He shifted the puck from his forehand to his backhand as he moved toward the net, then lifted it top shelf past Marc-Andre Fleury for a game-winner.

"The crossover and that explosiveness was generated from both his inside and outside edge," explains Derek Popke, a skating coach in Vancouver who works with multiple NHLers, including Bowen Byram and Sam Reinhart. "He generated power to push on his inside edge and then follow that push with his outside edge to cross under and then explode under the turn."

It was maybe his top highlight so far — maybe a goal of the year candidate — but just another example of the types of plays he makes regularly.

"Makar as a skater is actually sort of a model," says Barry Karn, a Minnesota-based skating coach who has worked for multiple NHL teams. "There isn't anything you wouldn't grade at the A level, let alone all the things you would grade at the A-plus level. He has just perfect balance on his skates."

Karn keeps the Chicago highlight on his phone to show skaters, and he uses multiple analogies for Makar's skating. The defenseman's elite balance and form help him glide across the ice, and Karn says that makes him look like someone running on an airport's moving walkway rather than running on the more-resistant carpet.

Makar's ability to keep control of the puck helps, too. In Karn's eyes, he's like a basketball player who doesn't have to dribble. He's able to move almost unencumbered by the puck and keep his head up, looking for playmaking opportunities across the ice.

"He can skate in a higher-number gear than other people can, and it's easy, it's efficient, for him," Karn says. "He's just traveling everywhere on the ice so much faster. Exponentially, really."

Popke also believes Makar maximizes his skating ability by maintaining good hand positioning and puck placement. Small details like that, he says, are what separate excellent players from exceptional ones.

When it comes to edgework, Makar says much of what he's able to do comes from opening his hips, allowing him to change directions quickly. Larkin is impressed by how the defenseman is able to gain speed while doing this, saying it reminds him of Sidney Crosby, the first player he remembers watching do it effectively.

"The new generation, Cale is probably the leader of that (with) how he moves his body to protect the puck while also building speed and buying space for himself to make plays," Larkin says.

His skating benefits him defensively, too. Larkin says Makar has gotten better at moving his feet to defend, and Popke notes that to stop elite skating forwards like Brad Marchand, defensemen have to be able to match their hip mobility and edgework.

"It's not about being a big burly defenseman back there," Popke says. "It's about mobility. And that's where the game is moving. It's about who can move."

Barbara Aidelbaum has coached skating for more than 40 years, working with the likes of Pavel Bure and Shea Theodore. She's never worked with Makar — Popke and Karn haven't, either — but has paid attention to his skating throughout his young career. She's impressed by his flexibility and, like Larkin, notes his hip mobility, which she says he showed during his overtime goal against Chicago.

"In order to do that at high speeds, you have to have really exceptional external rotation," she says. "Your hips have to be very flexible and you have to be able to turn your hips extremely fast. You don't just do that on the ice. That comes from your off-ice training."

Aidelbaum also calls attention to Makar's 180-degree pivot move, which he uses to evade defenders and create space. That comes from opening his hips, too.

As Aidelbaum says, off-ice training has played an essential role in Makar's skating development. Growing up, the defenseman loved to sprint for exercise and, during his two seasons at UMass, spent time in the weight room working on his explosiveness. He mentions squats, ladder drills and jumping exercises as workouts that played a role in his skating.

"(In) a lot of sports, you have that explosive nature through your feet," he says. "It's just kind of harnessing that and using that in the right areas. Now it's just maintaining that and making sure you don't lose your edge."

Makar never had skating-specific coaches growing up, though he did do power-skating training at hockey camps. He refined his creativity on outdoor rinks as a kid in Calgary, his dad, Gary, says, and his coaches let him play to his strengths.

"Even when I was young, it was pretty abnormal (for a defenseman) to be all over the ice," Cale says. "I was fortunate to have great coaches that allowed me to use my skating abilities and play

the game I want rather than just being that stay-at-home guy."

Coach Jared Bednar and the Avalanche let him play his game, too. It matches the direction the game is moving and is a huge part of what has made the team one of the NHL's top contenders.

"What he can do offensively, that's up to him," Coffey says. "He's certainly got the game to do it, the way the game is now. There's not a whole lot of physical play out there.

"Yeah, it's faster. But nobody's faster than him."

Bowen Byram

Inside Defenseman's Harrowing First Year With the Avalanche

By Peter Baugh

NOVEMBER 17, 2021

Bowen Byram was sick of it. Sick of thinking he was better, only for symptoms to return. Sick of not being able to put everything into his offseason training. Sick of not feeling like himself.

The Avalanche defenseman called his mom one day in summer 2021 when the load got too heavy. He had felt totally out of it skating that morning. Months of frustration — of setbacks and symptoms and not knowing what was wrong — had built up. When Stacey Byram answered, he confessed a growing worry: that his career was slipping away.

"What am I going to do now?" he remembers asking. "I can't play hockey anymore."

Sitting in his Toyota Tacoma in Vancouver, where he trains during the offseason, he was a worn-down 20-year-old, struggling and scared. He'd never suffered a serious injury before the 2020-21 season, but in his first full year as an NHL player, he's dealt with multiple concussions, vertigo and COVID-19, all of which have limited him to only 30 games.

At times over the summer, Byram didn't know what symptoms were caused by what. His medical situation was perplexing, and the recovery process hasn't been fun. The family thought at various times they were done with it, and then something else would go wrong.

Now, after it finally looked like he weathered the worst of his problems, an errant elbow has thrown him back on the roller coaster once again.

Byram, who often sports a youthful grin, is confident and chatty when he feels like himself. He's a jokester, someone who occasionally talked too much while growing up in Cranbrook, British Columbia, but was constantly kind, looking for ways to include classmates and teammates, his mom says. When New Jersey defenseman Ty Smith met Byram four years ago on Canada's U18 team, he couldn't believe how outgoing his new teammate was, and Avalanche forward Tyson Jost calls Byram bubbly, a "salt of the earth guy" who brings good banter to the dressing room.

"He's a social being," Stacey says. "He's touchy and interactive and wants to look in your eyes."

So the isolation of the COVID-19 pandemic posed challenges for Byram. He didn't appear in any games for the Avalanche in the 2020 playoffs but skated with the team in the Edmonton bubble, spending more than a month within the strict parameters there. Then, at Team Canada's training camp ahead of the World Junior Championship, he had to quarantine for 14 days in his hotel room after two teammates tested positive for the virus. He ultimately captained Canada to a silver medal and, in January 2021, arrived in Denver to join the Avalanche and take the first step in a lifelong dream: playing NHL games.

But the 2020-21 season was far from normal. Colorado instructed players to remain cautious of the virus, so there weren't the normal get-togethers or team outings. His parents weren't in the stands for his NHL debut; they watched from their couch in Cranbrook.

Byram, the people lover, spent his free time by himself, all while adjusting to being a young defenseman in the world's hardest league.

"Of course, he was ecstatic being down there," Stacey says. "(But) I could tell he was really lonely."

Then came the concussions. Byram doesn't know what caused the first one, which he sustained in a late-February game against Arizona. He just woke up the next morning not feeling right.

When the team diagnosed Byram with a concussion, Stacey decided she needed to be there. She drove 17 hours to Denver from Cranbrook, presenting a note from the team at the U.S.-Canada border saying she was coming to help her son.

Byram recovered fine from the first concussion, returning to the lineup 19 days later. But then, with the Avalanche hosting Vegas in late March, he found himself chasing a puck toward the side boards. As he flung the puck out of the defensive zone, Golden Knights forward Keegan Kolesar flew toward him, leaving his feet and making contact with Byram's head. The defenseman grabbed his helmet before skating off the ice and heading to the dressing room.

With fans not yet allowed in Ball Arena due to COVID-19 regulations, Stacey watched on TV from her son's apartment. She texted her husband, Shawn, after the play. They worried and waited, but the fear dissipated when Byram eventually returned to the game.

That relief faded as soon he got home.

"I could tell the minute he walked in it wasn't good," she says.

Byram was upfront with her, saying he didn't feel well but would go to bed and see how he was doing in the morning. When he woke up, there was no improvement. He felt foggy. Not like himself.

That hit began a yo-yo of progress and setbacks. Concussion recovery isn't linear, so at points Byram would feel better, only to hit another rut. He started dealing with vertigo, too.

"I'd be so dizzy, I'd be over the toilet almost throwing up," he says.

During times he felt up for it, Byram and Stacey would go for walks. They'd play cards or go for a drive, one time making a trip to Red Rocks to take in the sandstone formations.

On other days, Byram couldn't do much.

"I just wasn't really up for it most of the time, just because I was feeling not like myself," he says.

The Avalanche set him up with a sports psychologist, and that helped. He also took to meditating, using the Calm app on his iPhone almost daily, which allowed him to play guided audio tailored to specific situations, be it for when he was relaxing or getting to sleep.

"(It) helps you lift that weight you're feeling off your shoulders at times," Byram says. "I just felt like nothing was going my way. ... It was kind of an escape."

Ten days after the Kolesar hit, as Byram started feeling better, he joined the team on a four-game road trip, and Stacey headed back home to British

Columbia. But as he neared a return to game action, he dealt with a setback of a different kind: He tested positive for COVID-19 while the team was in Anaheim.

Byram took a car service back to Denver, sequestered in a taped-off backseat for 16 hours. He felt a little sick for a few days after his positive test, but it wasn't too bad. After going through protocol, he worked out a few times and — finally — got back on the ice.

That didn't go as planned.

"After I skated, I felt like I was a corpse," he says. "I was dizzy, couldn't see. It was crazy. It was like somebody was pounding on my head. It was tough, and everything snowballed on top of it."

His vertigo episodes became more frequent after he got COVID-19, and he didn't always know what was causing his symptoms. It was, as he put it, an undocumented area. One doctor told him that COVID-19 picks on weaker parts of the body.

"And Bowen's weak part at that time was his brain," his dad says. "We think it put him back a long way."

"If you have a head injury, then you get an illness that affects the neural system, you have all these side effects that nobody's really studied yet," says trainer Jordan Mackenzie, who worked with Byram over the summer.

With Byram's mom back in British Columbia, his girlfriend, Kailey, visited from Nova Scotia, where she's in college. He was frustrated with his situation and, like his mom had, his girlfriend provided moral support. Avalanche center Nathan MacKinnon also helped out, paying for Byram to work with his personal trainer, Marcin Goszczynski.

Goszczynski did functional neurology exercises with Byram, and the defenseman had an upswing ahead of the playoffs. The medical staff cleared him to play, but, while he skated with the team throughout the postseason, coach Jared Bednar didn't put him in the lineup. The coach hadn't been blown away with the games he'd seen Byram play earlier in the season, and he was hesitant to throw such a young player into a physical second-round playoff series against a strong Vegas team.

"Would've loved to have him back a few weeks before the season ended, be able to experiment with him a little bit, see how he played, and then he could've been a good option for us," Bednar says. "But he just wasn't healthy."

When the Avalanche lost Game 6, Byram watched his first NHL season end from the press box. He had pushed to get back in the lineup, but in retrospect, he believes it's good he didn't get into game action, because his situation took a turn south when summer training began.

"I just went downhill again and kind of fell apart," he says.

Byram arrived in Vancouver in mid-June, motivated for an offseason training with NHLers Brendan Gallagher, Milan Lucic and Ty Smith, only to feel the lingering effects of his injury return. Mackenzie, who has worked with Byram since 2018, noticed his recovery times were slower during workouts. He had less energy.

Mackenzie knows Byram as a loud guy, happy to talk with anyone and joke around with serious veterans like Lucic. But that aspect of his personality was lacking at the start of the summer. He normally loves skating and working out in the gym, but he physically couldn't put all his effort into it. That sucked out the enjoyment.

"I've just totally been invested since I can remember," Byram says. "I've always said I'm going to be a hockey player. That was the scary thing for me: not totally knowing what the future was going to hold."

He didn't necessarily feel terrible; just off. And the buildup of not feeling like himself led him to the call with his mom. Stacey's heart stopped when she heard how dejected he was.

"It was probably a bit over-reactive from myself, but when you're in positions like that and not feeling good, it really is hard to keep a positive mindset," Byram says.

Mentally and physically exhausted, he needed to vent, he remembers, and Stacey mostly just listened. She also gave him some perspective: Just

because he was injured then didn't mean he'd always be injured.

Mackenzie and Byram's goal for the summer was to get "Bo back to being Bo," the trainer says. That meant pouring time into treatment. The clinic he trained at in Vancouver had a massage therapist who worked on the soft tissue around his neck, and he saw a specialist with experience in post-concussion management. He tried to check every box, hoping for a breakthrough.

That also meant seeing a therapist in Vancouver. Byram says he wasn't depressed, but he felt on edge after months of frustration. He needed someone to help him take a step back.

"You don't want to admit something is wrong, but when something is wrong, it needs to be taken care of," he says. "I'm not afraid to tell anyone I saw a therapist now. I'm proud. I think everybody should. It helped me so much and it helped rejuvenate me as a person and eventually on the ice again."

He saw improvements and, at the end of July, went on a 10-day wilderness trip in the Yukon with his dad. They camped near Kusawa Lake, completely isolated and unplugged from the outside world. To get there, they had to drive more than 24 hours north and then, since drivable roads extend only so far, take a small plane into the bush.

"There's a lot of hardship and physical exertion and pain that goes with it," Shawn says. "You've got to be motivated by something you can't always explain."

Byram felt symptoms on a couple of days during the trip, his dad says, but he mostly just valued the grounding presence of nature. It was hard work — they hiked more than a dozen miles some days — but good for staying in the moment. On their last evening, with a plane set to come the next morning, father and son built a fire. Byram kicked off his shoes and sat against a rock, his toes near the warmth of the flames. There was a sense of exhaustion between them, and accomplishment, too.

"That (trip) kind of gave him — and I think his nervous system — a chance to really settle down and take in all the work that had been done over the past three or four weeks before he left," Mackenzie says.

When Byram returned to Vancouver after the trip, Mackenzie saw a shift. He radiated enthusiasm walking through the door. "Let's go!" the trainer thought to himself.

Bo was back to being Bo.

In November 2021, Byram glided toward the Columbus net on a two-on-one, sandy hair poking out of the back of his helmet. He waited calmly for a pass from teammate Nazem Kadri and, when it came, flicked the puck into the net. Not all defensemen have this type of offensive skill, especially at 20 years old, and Byram wasn't done. With less than a minute left in the game and the Avalanche trailing by a goal, he flung a shot on net and watched as it zipped in for a goal. He turned, full of adrenaline, and pumped his fist.

In that moment, it felt like a statement game, like Byram had arrived as a truly dangerous NHL player — maybe even a star. He showed all the tools that led Colorado to draft him at No. 4 in 2019, as well as confidence he believes he lacked during his 19-game stint in 2020-21.

"Every time I step on the ice and I feel good, it's such a breath of fresh air, because, seriously, for a while there, I was like, 'I'm done,'" he said at the time, noting that most of his lingering injury concern had dissipated.

A thought struck Stacey after she watched her son force overtime with the Blue Jackets. She felt like — after everything — the family had finally made it through. Sure, there had been scares since his return, notably when Byram took a dangerous cross-check into the boards against Minnesota, but her son had continually been fine. He told his mom about how good he was feeling: better than he'd felt since before his days as a major junior player in the Western Hockey League.

Then came the elbow.

With the Avalanche hosting the Canucks, Byram skated toward Vancouver captain Bo Horvat, ready to fight for a puck along the boards. As the two collided, Horvat's elbow hit Byram's face and the defenseman fell to the ice. He got up quickly but skated gingerly to the bench and went down to the dressing room.

An all-too familiar problem was back.

"It's scary stuff," teammate and close friend Alex Newhook says.

Byram felt great the morning after absorbing Horvat's elbow, and he skated with the team, laughing between drills like normal. But concussions are cruel and unpredictable. The next day, he woke up feeling not well. Within two days, the team had put him back in concussion protocol.

"That's not something you ever want to see," teammate Andre Burakovsky says.

Bednar doesn't have a return timeline, and how could he? He said that Byram is out until he feels better. Then, once again, he can begin the process of easing himself back into action.

Given the injury and Byram's history, it's unclear when that will come. ▬▬

'You Have to Give to Get'

Avalanche GM Joe Sakic Pays the Price to Bring in Needed Depth at Trade Deadline

By Peter Baugh

MARCH 21, 2022

t last season's trade deadline, general manager Joe Sakic made moves around the edges, acquiring the likes of Patrik Nemeth and Carl Soderberg without giving up much in return. But when the playoffs came around and Vegas tested Colorado's depth, the Avalanche didn't have enough.

Sakic seems to have learned his lesson.

"You have to give to get," he said Monday.

That's what he did over the past week, culminating with a push in the final hours ahead of the trade deadline. The Avalanche acquired Artturi Lehkonen from Montreal, giving up prospect Justin Barron and a 2024 second-round pick. They also added depth forward Andrew Cogliano from the Sharks for a 2024 fifth-round pick.

"(Lehkonen) was one of the guys we thought would be a great fit for the way we play, the way he plays, the need," said Sakic, who envisions the 26-year-old playing on rookie center Alex Newhook's wing. "The bottom six and our depth is much improved. To go through a two-month playoff run, you need depth."

Lehkonen has 29 points in 58 games this season with good underlying metrics, and one NHL scout praised it as a smart move. Sakic also likes the leadership he believes the team will get from Cogliano, who has played 1,122 career games.

Monday's pair of moves came after Colorado acquired Josh Manson and Nico Sturm last week from Anaheim and Minnesota, respectively. In total, the Avalanche's deadline looked like this:

IN: Josh Manson, Nico Sturm, Artturi Lehkonen and Andrew Cogliano
OUT: Tyson Jost, Justin Barron, Drew Helleson, a 2023 second-round pick, a 2024 second-round pick and a 2024 fifth-round pick

Manson and Sturm have already debuted for Colorado and have started playing on the penalty kill. They quickly fell in line with the team's vision: a long run this summer

"(Playoffs) suits my game a little bit — that in-your-face style, physical," said Manson.

"I want to help this team win the Stanley Cup," added Sturm, who adds defensive prowess and faceoff ability. "That's the goal."

Sakic traded away more chips than he did last season, but he also got more back in return.

"Every team is different," Sakic said. "There were deals to be made this year that really addressed what we thought we needed."

Lehkonen, the Avalanche's main addition Monday, comes with big-game experience. He ended Vegas' 2020-21 season with an overtime goal in Game 6 of the Western Conference final, and he was World Junior teammates with Mikko Rantanen. Rantanen was happy about the acquisition, he said on his way out of the arena.

Moving Barron marked a loss to the team's prospect pool, but Colorado viewed him as less untouchable than 2019 first-round picks Bowen Byram and Newhook. Sakic said the team likely wouldn't have moved the 2020 first-rounder for a rental, but Lehkonen is a pending restricted free agent, so Colorado has team control beyond this season.

The Avalanche also inquired about now-former Flyers captain Claude Giroux, the biggest name moved at the deadline. Talks didn't get far, though, because Giroux wanted to go to the Panthers and had a full no-movement clause.

"That was the place he wanted to go, so we didn't engage," Sakic said.

Along with the deadline additions, Colorado's roster could get another boost in the near future. Byram, who is recovering from a concussion, is now skating in a full-contact sweater, which Sakic called "a great sign."

"He'll let us know when he's ready to play, but I know that's his goal: to be able to come back and play," he said. "He needs more practice time and some games. It's all positive right now."

Defenseman Samuel Girard (lower body) should also be back by season's end, and captain Gabriel Landeskog is rehabbing from knee surgery. The team hopes he'll "have a couple games before the playoffs start," Sakic said.

If healthy, the Avalanche could roll into the playoffs with this lineup:

Gabriel Landeskog—Nathan MacKinnon—Mikko Rantanen

Valeri Nichushkin—Nazem Kadri—Andre Burakovsky

Artturi Lehkonen—Alex Newhook—J.T. Compher

Andrew Cogliano—Nico Sturm—Logan O'Connor

Devon Toews—Cale Makar
Samuel Girard—Josh Manson
Bowen Byram—Ryan Murray

Darcy Kuemper
Pavel Francouz

Other lineup options are Nicolas Aube-Kubel, Darren Helm, Kurtis MacDermid, Erik Johnson and Jack Johnson

"We were able to add to the depth of the group, and that's important," Sakic said. "We know great character guys are coming in to help our locker room and bring that winning attitude and try to win a Cup."

Sakic said after last deadline that the 2021 roster was "as deep a team as we're going to have." He might've found a way to make this year's group even deeper. ▬▬

Why the Avalanche Players Wear Their Numbers

From Jack Johnson's No. 3 to Mikko Rantanen's No. 96

By Peter Baugh

MARCH 25, 2022

Hockey uniforms don't allow much room for self-expression outside of one place: the back of the jersey.

For some players, the number they wear carries a story or tribute. For plenty, it was just a random assignment. For others, it speaks to superstitions.

The Athletic looked into how every Avalanche player — including the newcomers — wound up with their number. Here are the findings, along with some quick hits on each number's history since the team moved to Denver.

No. 3: Jack Johnson
"My dad actually played hockey and wore No. 3 at the University of Wisconsin. I started wearing No. 3 as a kid," Johnson said. "I didn't wear it in Columbus because Marc Methot had it and he was an older guy. I wasn't going to ask him for it. As soon as I could, I switched back."

Johnson is the eighth player in Avalanche history to wear No. 3. Chris Bigras (2016-18) wore it most recently before Johnson.

No. 4: Bowen Byram
Byram's dad, Shawn, said he liked single-digit numbers for defensemen, and when he coached, he encouraged it. Byram also wore No. 44 at points growing up.

Byram is the eighth player in Avalanche history to wear No. 4. Other notable players to wear it include Tyson Barrie, current TV analyst John Michael-Liles, current assistant Nolan Pratt, Hall of Famer Rob Blake and Uwe Krupp... who scored the Cup-clinching overtime goal in 1996. No. 4 is probably the most-accomplished non-retired number. Barrie (2014-19) wore it most recently before Byram.

No. 6: Erik Johnson
"It was actually at the U.S. Development Program," Johnson said. "The U18 team got all the numbers 1-30 and then the U17 got 30 and above. I was one of the last guys at the rink that day and No. 6 was one of the only numbers not taken, so I just stuck with it."

Johnson is the 10th player in Avalanche history to wear No. 6. Jonas Holos (2011) wore it most recently before Johnson.

No. 7: Devon Toews

Toews took No. 7 as a baseball player growing up, and he wore it in the AHL with the Bridgeport Islanders. He's had a couple other numbers in his career — No. 6 at Quinnipiac University and No. 25 with the Islanders — but they were taken by Johnson and Logan O'Connor, respectively, when Toews got to Colorado.

"I let OC keep (No. 25)," he said. "Maybe he'll get me a dinner at some point."

Toews is the 11th player in Avalanche history to wear No. 7. Kevin Connauton (2020) wore it most recently before Toews.

No. 8: Cale Makar

"I wore it back in junior," Makar said. "I didn't really get to pick when I got here. They just kind of gave it to me. I've always been No. 8 or 16. Can't go wrong with either."

Why those two numbers?

"Sixteen is a really unique D number," he said. "I feel like there aren't a lot of D out there who are 16. No. 8 is your classic number. Looks pretty sleek on the back."

Makar is the eighth player in Avalanche history to wear No. 8. If he continues on his current pace, he'll be the last. Joe Colborne (2017) wore it most recently before Makar.

No. 11: Andrew Cogliano

Cogliano, the newest member of the Avalanche, doesn't have a reason for No. 11 specifically, but he likes low numbers and has never worn anything above No. 17 in his NHL career.

"I'm old school," he said. "I'm not a high number guy."

Cogliano is the 13th player in Avalanche history to wear No. 11. Mikhail Maltsev (2021-22) and Matt Calvert (2019-21) wore it most recently before Cogliano.

No. 13: Valeri Nichushkin

Nichushkin wore No. 43 in Dallas because of his birthday (March 4). He preferred not to share why he changed to No. 13 in Colorado.

Nichushkin is the fifth player in Avalanche history to wear No. 13. Back in 1995, Valeri Kamensky wore the number when he scored the first goal in Avalanche history after the team moved from Quebec City. Alex Kerfoot (2018-19) wore it most recently before Nichushkin.

No. 16: Nicolas Aube-Kubel

"Someone gave it to me when I was really young," Aube-Kubel said. "I just kept with it. My grandpa really likes Henri Richard, the captain from Montreal who has the most Stanley Cup rings, so I thought it would be cool to have his number. But I never saw him play or anything. I didn't idolize him, but it was just cool."

He wore No. 62 in Philadelphia because No. 16 is retired (Bobby Clarke).

Aube-Kubel is the eighth player in Avalanche history to wear No. 16. Nikita Zadorov (2016-20) more it most recently before Aube-Kubel.

No. 18: Alex Newhook

Newhook always wore No. 8 growing up, but that changed when he played junior hockey with the Victoria Grizzlies in 2017-18. No. 8 was retired because Jordie Benn wore it, so Newhook was going to go with No. 16, his dad's old number. Unfortunately for him, that was retired because Jamie Benn wore it.

"So I went with No. 18 and really liked it," he said.

He has the Benn brothers to thank.

Newhook is the 11th player in Avalanche history to wear No. 18. Derick Brassard (2019) wore it most recently before Newhook.

No. 25: Logan O'Connor

"They gave me three options, and I liked 25 the most, and that is literally it," O'Connor said. "I have zero allegiance to any number. It doesn't bother me at all."

O'Connor is the seventh player in Avalanche history to wear No. 25. Mikhail Grigorenko (2016-17) wore it most recently before O'Connor.

No. 26: Jacob MacDonald

MacDonald, currently in the AHL with the Colorado Eagles, initially got assigned No. 34 the

training camp after the Avalanche traded for him. Then, when the team traded for Carl Soderberg last season, MacDonald gave up the number so the veteran could wear it.

The Avalanche offered MacDonald a few numbers as a replacement. "I think it was 10, 16 and 26 or something," he said. He picked No. 26 because his birthday is February 26, plus he has a few buddies who wear the number.

MacDonald is the fifth player in Avalanche history to wear No. 26. Most notably, Paul Stastny wore the number from 2007-14. Going back to the Nordiques days, Stastny's dad, Hall of Famer Peter Stastny, also wore the number. Andrew Agozzino (2019) wore it most recently before MacDonald.

No. 28: Ryan Murray

"They just said, 'Do you want 28?'" Murray said. "I said, 'Sure.'"

Easy enough.

Murray is the 11th player in Avalanche history to wear No. 28. Ian Cole (2018-21) wore it most recently before Murray.

No. 29: Nathan MacKinnon

"No. 22 was taken when I first came to the league," MacKinnon said. "That's what I wore in junior. I wore No. 9 growing up, so I just combined the two numbers."

He's happy with the number, he said. As a Calder Trophy winner and three-time Hart Trophy finalist, he's clearly had success with it.

MacKinnon is the fifth player in Avalanche history to wear No. 29 and almost certainly the last. Ryan Stoa (2009-11) wore it most recently before MacKinnon.

No. 35: Darcy Kuemper

Kuemper got assigned No. 35 when he was 10 or 11.

"Not much of a story to it," he said.

Kuemper is the 11th player in Avalanche history to wear No. 35. Jonas Johansson (2021) wore it most recently before Kuemper.

No. 37: J.T. Compher

"That's the number they gave me in training camp my first year."

Compher is the ninth player in Avalanche history to wear No. 37. Colin Smith (2015) wore it most recently before Compher.

No. 39: Pavel Francouz

"I've always loved the number 3," Francouz said. "Since I started playing pro, that one was taken. I decided to go with 33. That was my number until I signed with Colorado. Obviously, this number was taken (retired for Patrick Roy), so I decided to go 39 because Dominik Hasek played with this number and he was my childhood hero."

Francouz is the fifth player in Avalanche history to wear No. 39. T.J. Galiardi (2010-12) wore it most recently before Francouz.

No. 42: Josh Manson

Manson is one of the newest Avalanche players, acquired at the trade deadline from Anaheim. His number goes back to his younger days with the Ducks. Initially, though, the team gave him No. 83 for his first training camp.

"I came back two or three years later, and I think I developed quite a bit, and my number went from 83 to 42," he said. "So either they lost my number and forgot about me and gave me 42 or I moved up and my number got better. ... I was always too scared to ask to change my number, so I left it and it became my own. Coming here, they were like, 'Do you want 42?' I went, 'Sure, why not?'" It's been with me for eight years now. Why change?"

Manson is the fifth player in Avalanche history to wear No. 42. Samuel Henley (2017) wore it most recently before Manson.

No. 43: Darren Helm

Helm got his number in training camp when he came into the league with the Detroit Red Wings.

"Ended up winning a Stanley Cup with it," he said. "Couldn't change it then, not changing it now."

Helm is the eighth player in Avalanche history to wear No. 43. Michael Sgarbossa (2013-15) wore it most recently before Helm.

No. 49: Samuel Girard

Girard wore No. 94 in Nashville, but Andrei Mironov had the number when he came to Colorado, so he switched the digits around.

"I just like the four and the nine," he said.

Girard is the second player in Avalanche history to wear No. 49. Serge Aubin (1999-00) wore it most recently before Girard.

No. 56: Kurtis MacDermid

The Kings gave MacDermid No. 56 when he broke into the league, and he has kept it since.

"It suits me," he said.

MacDermid is the second player in Avalanche history to wear No. 56. Marko Dano (2019) wore it most recently before MacDermid.

No. 62: Artturi Lehkonen

Lehkonen, a deadline acquisition, has worn No. 62 since he was a kid because his dad, Ismo, was born in 1962.

Lehkonen is the fourth player in Avalanche history to wear No. 62. Chris Wagner (2015-16) wore it most recently before Lehkonen.

No. 78: Nico Sturm

Sturm had a journey getting to No. 78. He wore No. 7 in Minnesota, but Toews already had that number in Colorado. No. 77 is retired for Ray Bourque, so he couldn't go that route, and Makar wears No. 8, the next number up. Sturm wore No. 17 playing college hockey at Clarkson, but he didn't want to take that number after getting traded this month for Tyson Jost, who wore it for the Avalanche.

So he sought out help.

"I asked my family and little brother: 'I'm kind of running out of ideas here,'" he said.

His brother suggested No. 78. Why? Their hometown team in Germany, Augsburger EV, was founded as a skating club in 1878.

"I thought it was a nice tribute to them," Sturm said.

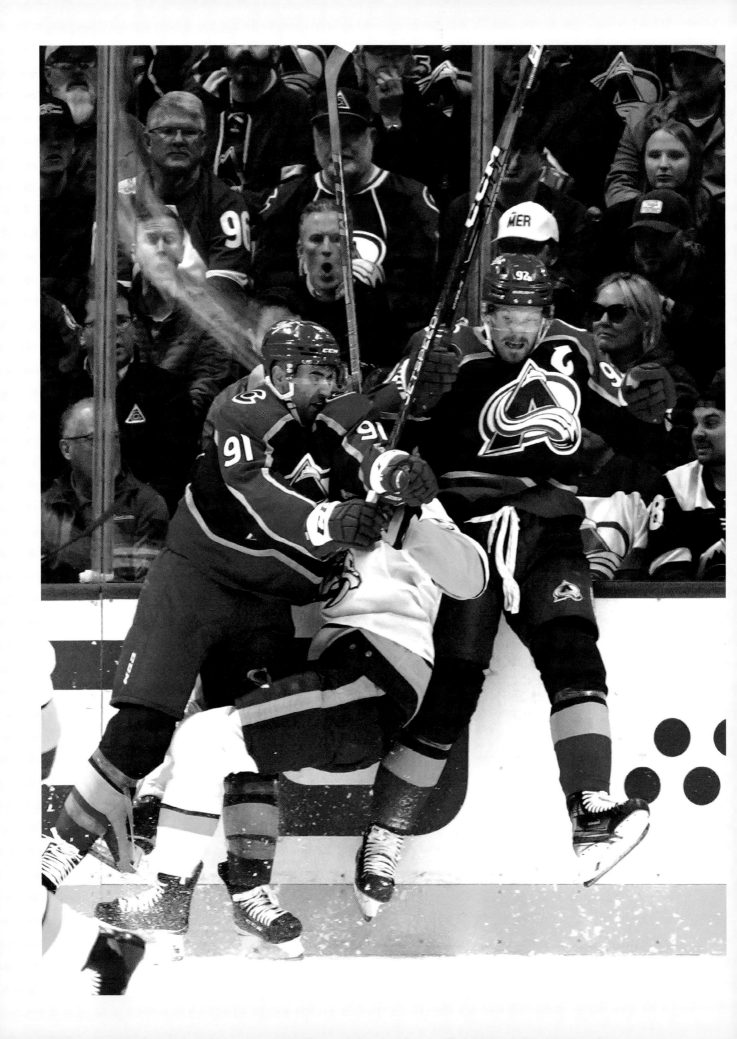

Sturm is the first player in Avalanche history to wear No. 78.

No. 91: Nazem Kadri

Kadri always liked No. 9 growing up, and he switched between No. 19 and No. 91 in his junior hockey days.

"I always had the nine in there," he said.

But when he got to the NHL with Toronto, he wore No. 43.

"(Brian Burke) was the (general) manager and he wouldn't let anyone go past a certain number," Kadri said. "I was a rookie. I wasn't about to fight him."

When he got traded to Colorado, he figured he'd go back to No. 91.

"Start a new chapter in my pro career," he said.

Kadri is only the second player in Avalanche history to wear No. 91. Vladislav Kamenev (2018-19) wore it most recently before Kadri.

No. 92: Gabriel Landeskog

The captain picked No. 92 because of his birth year, 1992.

Landeskog is the first player in Avalanche history to wear No. 92. If his number is retired, he'll go down as the only.

No. 95: Andre Burakovsky

Burakovsky wore No. 95 in the OHL playing in Erie, where he was teammates with Connor McDavid and Kurtis MacDermid.

"I guess because (1995) was my birth year," he said. "I was having a good year, and then I came to Washington and they gave me 65 in training camp, and I was playing really good in training camp with 65."

But he didn't find as much success as he wanted in Washington, so he returned to No. 95 when traded to the Avalanche.

"I had to change back and try something that works," he said.

Burakovsky is the first player in Avalanche history to wear No. 95.

No. 96: Mikko Rantanen

Rantanen wears No. 96 because it's his birth year. Sidney Crosby was Rantanen's favorite player growing up, and Crosby wears No. 87 for his birth year.

Rantanen is the first player in Avalanche history to wear No. 96. He's another candidate for an eventual retired number. ▬

Artturi Lehkonen

From a Hahl Jersey to a Rantanen Connection,
a Match Decades in the Making

By Peter Baugh

APRIL 8, 2022

Colorado may have only acquired Artturi Lehkonen at the trade deadline, but the left winger got his first gear from the club two decades ago.

After the Avalanche lost the 2001-02 Western Conference final to the Red Wings, center Riku Hahl returned to his native Finland for the offseason. While back home, he visited Ismo Lehkonen, one of his old coaches, and brought gifts: a Patrick Roy Avalanche hat for Ismo's 6-year-old son, Artturi, as well as one of Hahl's own No. 32 jerseys, signed by Colorado teammates. Hahl then spent hours out back playing street hockey with Artturi, who'd already taken a fascination with the sport.

So when Avalanche general manager Joe Sakic — Hahl's captain for all three of his NHL seasons — traded for Lehkonen hours before the March 21 deadline, Hahl reached out to Ismo, reminding him of how close he came to a Cup Final with the Avalanche.

"Now Artturi has to finish the job," he told his former coach.

The 26-year-old Lehkonen was Colorado's biggest trade deadline acquisition — a well-rounded player Sakic hoped would take his team from Stanley Cup contention to a Stanley Cup championship. He's a two-way, middle-six forward who can complement the team's high-end offensive stars.

When Colorado got Lehkonen from Montreal, management told Avalanche coach Jared Bednar he was getting a 5-foot-11 version of Valeri Nichushkin, one of the team's top forecheckers and a force in all situations. Through four games with his new club, Lehkonen has lived up to that billing, earning more than 17 minutes of ice time in each of the past three Avalanche contests.

"He's relentless, eh?" Bednar said after his team beat the Penguins on Saturday.

Considering Lehkonen's personality and influences growing up, it's easy to see why.

———————— ————————

Before Artturi could walk, he was shooting one-timers.

In the Lehkonen family home in Turku, Finland, Ismo set up a small net in the living room, and he bought small sticks that young Artturi — nicknamed Arsi — could use. The smiling baby would crawl around holding a stick, swiping at balls Ismo rolled his way.

"He was already having fun," Ismo says.

Ismo played professional hockey in Finland and coached in the nation's highest league, and his five children all played different sports. Artturi's oldest sister, Iina, for example, made Finland's top league in pesäpallo, the country's version of baseball, and now plays padel, a racket sport. Artturi, the middle child, tried multiple sports, including soccer, basketball and tennis.

None gripped him like hockey. Ismo remembers showing Artturi VHS tapes of professional players, including the "Legion of Doom" line in Philadelphia. When he was around nine years old, Artturi also enjoyed breaking down film of his Ismo's team. He'd barrage the coach with questions.

"Why did you pick this clip?" Ismo remembers Arturri asking. "Why are they doing that? What's the problem here?"

When Ismo thinks of his son growing up, he also thinks of someone who hated losing. It didn't matter if he was with his hockey team, out on the street with friends or simply playing games with his family. He couldn't stand coming up short.

"When he was really young, he (would) run into the woods and cry," Ismo says.

His dad tried to teach him what he called the five-minute rule. After a loss, you can let yourself feel upset and reflect for a short period of time, but then you have to move on. That's how Finnish legend and Hockey Hall of Famer Teemu Selanne would approach things, Ismo would tell Artturi.

"I don't think he's learned that 100 percent now," Ismo says. "But he's getting better and better at handling those situations."

And there are worse types of players than ones who hate losing.

—————— A ——————

During his early teenage years, Lehkonen met a hockey player from Nousiainen, Finland, a town just outside of Turku. The kid, a blonde-haired forward named Mikko Rantanen, was a year younger than Lehkonen, so they only played on the same team at tournaments every once in a while.

But Lehkonen remembers his now-Avalanche teammate, describing him in a way few would today: tiny. And then the growth spurt came.

"I was taller than him, then one summer later he was towering over me," Lehkonen says. "It was quite weird."

Lehkonen went on to compete at world juniors with the 6-foot-4 Rantanen, one of his favorite players to watch in the league. The Colorado star carries similar respect for Lehkonen.

"He's one of the smarter players I know, defensively and offensively," Rantanen says. "Exactly what we need."

Both players' skill sets became appealing to NHL teams, and the Canadiens drafted Lehkonen at No. 55 in 2013. But before heading to North America, Lehkonen played two years with Frolunda in Sweden, where coach Roger Rönnberg pushed him to improve defensively. He had his young forward kill penalties and focus on forechecking, telling him that's what would make him successful in the NHL. Sure enough, both are now strong aspects of his game.

Lehkonen came to Montreal in 2016-17, and his work ethic immediately impressed veteran teammate Tomas Plekanec, who became one of his mentors and friends. His stick placement jumped out, as did his skating ability and body positioning.

"I was a player who paid attention to details," Plekanec says. "He came in, and being as young as he was, he was already at that stage. That really caught my eye."

The two would go out to dinner on the road — teammates chirped them for their early meal times — and Plekanec offered advice for navigating the hockey-crazed Montreal market. His biggest tip is something easier said than done: Don't let outside voices distract you. Lehkonen took the advice well; Plekanec didn't have to share it twice, the now-39-year-old remembers.

Canadiens defenseman Joel Edmundson says everyone on the team loved Lehkonen, and former linemate Phillip Danault, now with the Kings, describes him as both humble and funny.

Lehkonen scored 149 career points in 396 games with the Canadiens — Plekanec believes he can improve his finishing, considering the chances he creates — and he played in at least 80 percent of games each of his seasons in Montreal. He also helped the Canadiens reach the playoffs in three of his five full seasons with the club.

"He has one of the best sticks defensively that I've seen," Danault says. "I think he's more known for that, killing penalties, but as he's shown, he can score the big goals, too."

None were bigger than the one he scored against Vegas during the 2021 playoffs. Leading the conference finals 3-2, Montreal hosted the Golden Knights for a crucial Game 6. The Canadiens' run to that point was already a miracle, considering they had a 24-21-11 record in the regular season, and excellent goaltending from Carey Price got them to overtime in Game 6.

Less than two minutes into the extra period, Lehkonen watched as an Alec Martinez slap shot bounced off Price's shoulder. Brendan Gallagher snatched the loose puck, leading the Canadiens in transition. Gallagher fed Danault in the neutral zone, and as he neared the net, the center whipped a backhanded pass to a charging Lehkonen.

Lehkonen threw his hands through the puck, sending it past goaltender Robin Lehner. Just like that, the Canadiens were going to the Stanley Cup Final for the first time since 1993.

"Seeing how hard he works and how well prepared he is, I'm so happy that it paid off for him," says Plekanec, who retired from the NHL in 2018.

Lehkonen leapt three times with joy behind the net, and Danault pulled him in for a hug. The rest of the Canadiens spilled onto the ice, half mobbing Lehkonen, half mobbing Price. Donning a red suit, Marc Bergevin, then the team's general manager, rushed to the bench and kissed the top of Lehkonen's head. Meanwhile, throngs of fans celebrated outside the arena.

"I guess it was a special goal," Lehkonen says.

That's an understatement. It was the biggest goal for the Canadiens in nearly 30 years, one that will always keep Lehkonen in Montreal's heart. Lehkonen says people frequently approached him about the goal in Montreal.

The Canadiens' deep playoff run didn't end with the ultimate prize, and the team has had a disastrous 2021-22 campaign, complete with injuries, Bergevin's firing and a coaching change. By the trade deadline, the Canadiens were sellers, and Lehkonen, a pending restricted free agent, became one of their most appealing trade chips. He knew speculation surrounded him, but as Plekanec taught him early in his career, he tuned it out as best he could.

"I was pretty used to it, to be honest," he says. "It wasn't the first time my name being in the rumors. It comes with the territory."

Plus, he jokes, he couldn't understand most of the trade talk in Montreal. He doesn't speak French.

At 1 p.m. on deadline day, Lehkonen put his head down for a pregame nap. He expected to suit up with his Montreal teammates that evening to take on Boston.

Twenty minutes later, his phone rang, jolting him awake. Canadiens general manager Kent Hughes was on the line, telling him he'd been traded to the Avalanche.

"It was kind of weird emotions," a tired Lehkonen said the day after the trade. "(There) was excitement but then it was like, 'What do I do now? What do I have to do?' I had to start packing and stuff.

"It was a hectic 24 hours."

Rantanen, who trains with Lehkonen in the off-season, was thrilled when he heard the news, and he immediately sent his friend a text. In Montreal, meanwhile, coach Martin St. Louis was "absolutely crestfallen" to lose Lehkonen, The Athletic's Pierre LeBrun reports, and Canadiens players also speak highly of their no-longer teammate.

"He can play first line if you want, put the points up, or he can play fourth line and only penalty kill," Edmundson says. "He's a utility player, a Swiss Army knife."

The fact that Lehkonen is so useful meant he didn't come cheap. The Avalanche had to part with a second-round pick as well as 2020 first-round pick Justin Barron, one of their top prospects. Sakic admitted it was hard to give Barron up, and the team wouldn't have done it if Lehkonen were a rental player.

Lehkonen had to miss three games waiting for immigration paperwork to go through, and he was rusty in his first Avalanche game, a 2-1 road win in Calgary. But he settled in, impressing his

new teammates and Bednar. The coach played him on the top line with Rantanen and Nathan MacKinnon for part of a game, and he found success on a line with Nichushkin. He scored his first goal with the club against the Penguins, potting an empty-netter in the third period.

Before Lehkonen ended the Golden Knights' 2021 season, the Avalanche fell to Vegas in the second round of the playoffs. Ismo says his son immediately noticed the focus around this year's Avalanche club. The players haven't forgotten the bitter end to last season. They're on a mission.

"Awesome team," Ismo says. "Everybody is doing their job, up and down."

Plus, they have been winning, and that's what Artturi likes most. ▬▬

Nazem Kadri

After Heartbreaking End to Toronto Run, Maturing Center Embraces Opportunity With Avalanche

By Peter Baugh

APRIL 27, 2022

Ashley Kadri was in the midst of her nesting phase, folding tiny clothes and tucking them into drawers. Thirty-seven weeks pregnant, she had just had her new condo decorated, completing the baby room with pink polka-dotted wallpaper. Baby Naylah's life was set to begin in Toronto, where her dad, Nazem, played hockey.

The expecting couple was on the couch watching TV when Nazem's phone rang. He doesn't normally leave the room for calls — only when his dad or his agent is on the line. So Ashley knew something was serious when he stood up and walked to the den to take the call.

She didn't have to wait long to find out what was going on. Leafs general manager Kyle Dubas kept Nazem on the phone for less than a minute — hurtfully short, in the forward's mind — to tell him he'd been traded from a city and team he didn't want to leave.

"Where are we going?" Ashley remembers asking.

Colorado. But first, Nazem went to their bedroom, shutting the door behind him. Ashley waited, giving him space until she saw a post pop up on Instagram. Nazem had written a thank you message to the city of Toronto. "You asked for my heart and I gave you my soul," he typed.

After seeing the post, Ashley opened the door to find Nazem on their bed. She could tell he was holding back tears. He was shocked. Heartbroken.

"It sucks, you know?" Ashley says. "It doesn't suck now, but when it was happening, it sucked."

The cause of the trade was no mystery. It came down to one play: a retaliatory cross-check to Bruins forward Jake DeBrusk's head in Game 2 of the Leaf's 2019 first-round series with Boston. That play led to Kadri's second suspension in as many postseasons, this time a five-gamer that kept him out through Game 7.

He never played another game for the Leafs. The team lost the series and lost faith in Kadri.

"Normally trades don't happen like that," Ashley says. "It's just a trade and it is what it is. But Naz got traded because he got suspended back-to-back. That's probably what it was."

The DeBrusk cross-check did more than cause a trade. It also cemented Kadri's reputation, one he's still trying to shed three years later.

Emotionally, moving on from Toronto prompted what Ashley calls a psychological resurgence in Nazem. For the first time, she says, he had to look inside himself and abandon his ego. It was comfortable, especially because the consequences of his actions rippled well beyond himself and even his team. It impacted his family, too. The trade forced Ashley and Naylah — who was born on July 7, 2019, six days after the trade — to move 1,500 miles to a new country and a new life.

Nazem's older sister, Yasmine, is a teacher in their hometown of London, Ontario, and she still hears things. Just this season, while walking through the halls, she overheard a Grade 8 student ask his teacher if Nazem was her brother. "He's always the one that gets kicked out of the games," the student said.

"I think in his mind, he was like, 'I don't want to ever put myself or my teammates through that (again), but I don't want to put my family through that, either,'" Ashley says.

It hasn't all gone according to plan. His 2021 postseason ended with yet another suspension, this one after a high hit that left St. Louis defenseman Justin Faulk unconscious on the ice. Blues players were livid. Brayden Schenn told reporters after the game that Kadri "can't control himself," and Ryan O'Reilly called for a suspension.

Kadri, meanwhile, insists he was trying to make a hockey play but missed his hit, and the Avalanche supported him through an unsuccessful appeal process. Coach Jared Bednar, for one, sees it as a different situation than his Toronto suspensions. This wasn't retaliatory. He didn't lose his cool.

"I've seen Naz grow up and try and be real intentional about what he does and try to stay disciplined," Bednar says. "He just missed his check by a couple of inches."

Colorado lost to Vegas in the second round, falling in Game 6, one game before Kadri was eligible to return from his eight-game suspension. He could've been a difference maker in a series in which the Avalanche desperately needed one.

But general manager Joe Sakic stood by Kadri, ignoring cries to trade the center ahead of this season. Kadri has validated Sakic's faith this year, posting the best numbers of his career. He's set to be an unrestricted free agent following the season and due a major raise, whether he stays in the city he's grown to love or heads elsewhere.

First, though, come playoffs, the beast that's brought out both the best and worst in him.

Sam Kadri was working at his furniture shop when his son, Nazem, was born. "Quick delivery," he says. As he drove to the hospital to join his wife, Sue, Tom Cochrane's song "Big League" came on the radio.

My boy's going to play in the big league
My boy's going to turn some heads
My boy's going to play in the big league
My boy's going to knock 'em dead

The ballad has a sad ending — the prospect in the song dies in a car accident — but the lyrics about the kid's promise are what stood out to Sam. The song finished right before he parked at the hospital, and he insists that, from that moment, he knew his son would make it to the NHL.

Sam, one of seven children, moved with his family from Lebanon to London, Ontario, when he was 4. His dad was a custodian and his mom looked after the kids, so money was tight. That left hockey out of the question. He watched as his friends joined teams and swore that, if he had kids, he'd put them in the sport.

Nazem, who grew up rooting for the Montreal Canadiens, started skating at 3 years old, and Sam, who became the owner of an auto repair shop, lied about his age so he could get on a team at age 4.

London, located nearly equidistant between Detroit and Toronto, is a city of 400,000 and home of Western University. The major junior team, the London Knights, play in front of nearly 10,000 fans. Joe Thornton, Logan Couture, Nick Suzuki and Drew Doughty — one of Kadri's linemates when he was 6 — are from the London area. Patrick Kane and Corey Perry played for the Knights. The walls of Joe Kool's, a local sports bar, are covered with hockey photos, many from Perry's 2005 Memorial Cup-winning team, which Nazem remembers watching as a teenager. He spent "more than a couple" great nights at Joe Kool's, where the food is good and the bartenders take care of you.

"It's kind of a small town vibe where everyone's friends with everybody," he says.

Nazem was a jokester growing up. He made his four sisters laugh with Will Ferrell impersonations and loved quoting movies. The Kadris watched a film every Friday night, becoming platinum members at their local Blockbuster. He was also ultracompetitive. He and his buddies had pool basketball games in the Kadris' backyard, which close friend Jason McNeill describes as "all-out war." They'd play street hockey, too, stopping only when they needed to replace the rollerblade wheels they'd burned through.

At A.B. Lucas Secondary School, multiple pictures of Kadri hang on the walls near the athletic department, and there's a plaque dedicated to him in the Hall of Honour. High school sports aren't as big of a deal in Canada as they are in the U.S., but Kadri spent a year on the basketball team, and he led the Lucas hockey team to a city championship in 2005. He still calls it one of his fondest sports memories.

"It wasn't the best hockey in the world," coach Tim Orr says. "But it sure was important."

The Kadris are practicing Muslims, and Nazem's dark skin stood out in Canadian rinks. He first heard a slur directed at him when he was around 11 or 12, playing in a game. He remembers that the words didn't come from a player. They came from an opposing parent.

"That's just a little something that happened here and there," he says. "Definitely more than you think."

He heard it when he played major junior in the Ontario Hockey League, too. With guidance from his dad, he learned how to ignore words he never should have had to hear.

Kadri played for the Kitchener Rangers, where now-Vegas coach Pete DeBoer drafted him, and then for the London Knights. Mark Hunter, who coached him with the Knights, remembers Kadri's blend of skill and physicality. He says his hits were so forceful that opponents' equipment flew everywhere.

"That's what makes him even better: He has that element," Hunter says. "As long as he doesn't cross that line. We all know that."

By the time Kadri left home for Kitchener at 15, NHL buzz had begun. Sure enough, with Montreal hosting the 2009 draft, Toronto picked him at No. 7. Sam, wearing a black shirt and a wide grin, pulled him in for a hug first. "I'm proud of you, buddy," he said in his son's ear. His boy was going to the big leagues. Sue kissed Nazem on the cheek. "I love you. I love you," she repeated, then pulled out her camcorder to film him walking onto the stage.

As Nazem lifted a royal blue Maple Leafs jersey over his head for the first time, the crowd full of Canadiens fans booed.

"Nice warm welcome here in Montreal," he joked in his post-draft TV interview.

———————— ————————

A few years into his Maple Leafs tenure, shortly after his rookie contract ended, Kadri sat in the passenger seat of his sports car. Colin Martin, a longtime friend, was driving through downtown Toronto, and he pulled to a stop at a red light. Suddenly, a man started knocking on Kadri's tinted window, which he somehow managed to see through. They both wondered for a second if the man was trying to rob them. Then they heard, "Kadri! Kadri!"

"It just goes to show you how those fans are," Martin says. "They love their Leafs."

Hollywood has movie stars. Toronto has hockey players.

Kadri remembers some fans almost fainting with excitement when he met them. His friends doubled as bodyguards when they went out, huddling around him and swatting phone cameras away. In 2016, a couple named their newborn girl "Kadri."

The city was a pressure cooker, and Kadri loved it.

He sat courtside at Raptors games. He got car endorsements. Leafs superfan Justin Bieber wished him a happy birthday on Twitter. Sure, he says, privacy was an occasional issue, but he enjoyed meeting new people and hearing their stories.

"He lived and breathed Toronto," Ashley says.

And Toronto kept a watchful eye, for better or worse. He took heat for his body weight early in his career. When fans found out he was dating Ashley, she deleted her Instagram account because of the number of comments. Tickets were in such high demand and Kadri got only two free ones per game, so Ashley says he would end up spending approximately $20,000 every season on tickets for friends and family.

"Any kid who plays in Toronto or Montreal, they should get paid more money, because they've got to put up with so much more crap," Sam says.

Kadri plays with emotion, and Leafs coaches credited him with often dragging the team into the action. He says he performs best when he has an edge to his game, and he's never afraid to get into scrums. But that's not the man Ashley knows off the ice, and almost all in-game animosity with opponents vanishes away from the rink. Just ask Mark Giordano. In February 2016, the then-Flames defenseman hit Kadri high, and the forward was livid by the time he got to the bench. He made a throat slashing gesture at Giordano that earned him a $5,000 fine.

That offseason, Nazem and Ashley saw Giordano outside a club in Toronto. Giordano asked Kadri to help him get inside, and he happily obliged. Their groups hung out together that night, running up an expensive tab. Giordano footed the bill at the end of the evening. "I've got it," Ashley remembers him saying. "You took that fine because of me." Giordano, now on the Leafs, even went to Nazem and Ashley's wedding in 2018.

Kadri had a good run with the Maple Leafs, logging 357 points in 561 games and helping them emerge as a consistent playoff team. But the pair of post-season suspensions marred the end of his time in the city.

"It's just so frustrating, to be honest," Ashley says. "I think he's never going to be able to get away from that reputation now."

After his last season in Toronto, Kadri told his mom he thought he was safe, showing her a message from Dubas telling him how much he appreciated him. But then, while he and Ashley were at Queen's Plate Race Track, Kadri got a call from his agent. The Leafs wanted to trade him to Calgary, a team he had on his no-trade list. Kadri considered accepting the trade, but he decided against it solely because he thought it would increase his chances of staying in Toronto.

Obviously, it didn't. Sakic worked out a deal to acquire a package headlined by Kadri, sending Toronto defenseman Tyson Barrie, forward Alex Kerfoot and a 2020 sixth-round draft pick.

"All he can do is show him what they lost," Ashley says. "I can't see Kyle Dubas sitting back thinking this was one of the better trades in his career."

Shortly after the trade rocked Kadri's world, his life changed again. Ashley went into labor, giving birth to Naylah, now a smiley 2-year-old who has developed a passion for going to the carwash with her parents.

"It kind of put life into perspective," Ashley says.

Sure, Nazem wasn't staying in Toronto. But he had a beautiful, healthy child. What could matter more than that?

Still, the transition had hurdles. Heartbreak lingered from leaving Toronto, where he was always a couple of hours from family. But a friendly gesture from Barrie, his trade counterpart, made moving a little easier. After the trade, the two players rented each other's homes, and Barrie left behind a basket full of Devil's Food Bakery goods and pamphlets of what to do in Denver. Kadri

liked his new teammates, and over the course of the COVID-19 pandemic, the family enjoyed being in a sunny city. They could eat outside and ride their bikes around Washington Park.

"Obviously, when (the Leafs trade) happened, it was a bit of a bitter situation," Kadri said during the Avalanche's road trip to Toronto in December 2021. "But it ended up being a little bit bittersweet."

Denver marked a new beginning, especially with Naylah entering his life. Nazem's sister Yasmine says the now-toddler has softened him. He's affectionate, picking her up and giving her kisses. She came down to the glass before a recent game, and her baba skated over, blowing her a kiss and repeatedly telling her how much he loved her. "He's obsessed," says Rema, one of his three younger sisters.

And his loved ones see increased maturity.

"You want to make the right decisions because your decisions affect her, too," Ashley says. "Whether it's making the decision not to go out with the boys or to come home at 11 p.m. after dinner rather than going out afterwards until 3, you have to take your kid into consideration."

The city has a much different feel than Toronto. Shortly after the trade, a reporter in Denver mistook Kadri for Pierre-Edouard Bellemare, a mistake that never would have happened while he was on the Maple Leafs. McNeil and their childhood buddies make fun of him for rarely getting recognized on the streets. "That must kill you," they'll say. And Ashley remembers him mentioning how much faster he can get out of the dressing room postgame. Interviews don't last nearly as long.

Kadri's growth in his new home made his 2021 postseason suspension even harder. He and his family saw it not as retaliatory but as a hockey play gone wrong. Sam remembers feeling numb after the hit, and Nazem and Ashley struggled to sleep in the following days. An appeal didn't lessen the eight-game suspension, and Kadri's season ended with him watching, not playing.

"Obviously, I strongly disagree (with the appeal decision), but what are you going to do?" he says. Once again came a wave of criticism. He received messages on Instagram laced with racist slurs. One called him "osama bin kadri." These are the type of insults Kadri has grown accustomed to and the type of language he wants to get rid of as a founding member of the Hockey Diversity Alliance, which started in the summer of 2020 with a mission to "eradicate systemic racism and intolerance in hockey."

Kadri returned to Toronto to train this offseason, and between the playoff suspension and his expiring contract, he entered 2021-22 with plenty to play for. And though his dad doesn't believe that has factored into his play this year, Nazem conceded in the preseason that he "maybe had a little chip on my shoulder."

"I know Naz just wants to play his heart out for this team and really wants to win the Cup this year for Colorado," Ashley says. "He really feels like, unlike Toronto, the Avs and Joe Sakic and Bednar gave him another chance."

So far he's kept his edge without crossing any lines. With 85 points through late April, he's already more than 20 ahead of his previous career high. For the first time in his career, he'll finish a season averaging more than a point per game, and he represented the Avalanche at the All-Star Game.

"What I'm excited about with Kadri is his commitment on the defensive side of things," Bednar said earlier in the season. "I don't think it's a coincidence that he's putting up points and producing the way he is because he's playing much better defensively."

Still, frustrations linger with how he's officiated. He was angry after an early-season game when he got an offsetting penalty with Blues goalie Jordan Binnington despite the fact that the goalie swung his stick at Kadri. "I'm getting misconducts for just talking now," he said. And in Carolina, captain Gabriel Landeskog vented about Nino Niederreiter getting away with a hook on Kadri.

"Whether a guy has been suspended numerous times or not, is he going to be carrying around that heavy baggage forever?" Landeskog said.

To some extent, maybe. But he can go a long way toward changing any lingering negative perception of him with more drama-free production like this season's.

Doing it on a postseason stage would be a good start. ▬▬

PLAY

FIRST ROUND
VS. NASHVILLE PREDATORS

GAME 1: AVALANCHE 7, PREDATORS 2

GAME 2: AVALANCHE 2, PREDATORS 1 (OT)

GAME 3: AVALANCHE 7, PREDATORS 3

GAME 4: AVALANCHE 5, PREDATORS 3

SECOND ROUND
VS. ST. LOUIS BLUES

GAME 1: AVALANCHE 3, BLUES 2 (OT)

GAME 2: BLUES 4, AVALANCHE 1

GAME 3: AVALANCHE 5, BLUES 2

GAME 4: AVALANCHE 6, BLUES 3

GAME 5: BLUES 5, AVALANCHE 4 (OT)

GAME 6: AVALANCHE 3, BLUES 2

OFFS

**WESTERN CONFERENCE FINAL
VS. EDMONTON OILERS**

GAME 1: AVALANCHE 8, OILERS 6

GAME 2: AVALANCHE 4, OILERS 0

GAME 3: AVALANCHE 4, OILERS 2

GAME 4: AVALANCHE 6, OILERS 5 (OT)

**STANLEY CUP FINAL
VS. TAMPA BAY LIGHTNING**

GAME 1: AVALANCHE 4, LIGHTNING 3 (OT)

GAME 2: AVALANCHE 7, LIGHTNING 0

GAME 3: LIGHTNING 6, AVALANCHE 2

GAME 4: AVALANCHE 3, LIGHTNING 2 (OT)

GAME 5: LIGHTNING 3, AVALANCHE 2

GAME 6: AVALANCHE 2, LIGHTNING 1

The Legend Grows

Cale Makar Steps Up, Lifts Avalanche to a Game 2 Win

By Peter Baugh

MAY 6, 2022

Sometimes in playoff hockey, a team simply outplays another and wins. Sometimes games change on the whims of a rubber disk, and sometimes games change on the whims of a third-string goalie having the night of his life. Other times, like Thursday night, a generational player finds a way to lift his team when the lights get brightest.

Cale Makar is mild-mannered. Kind but reserved. He read six books a semester his sophomore year at UMass, researching leadership and self-understanding in independent study classes. He's not flashy — at least not until he's on the ice. But when he plays hockey, he's explosive, a force earning praise from giants of the game, whether it's Nicklas Lidstrom or Paul Coffey or Ray Bourque. Even Wayne Gretzky — The Great One — couldn't help but rave about Makar's skating during the national broadcast of Game 2 of the Avalanche-Predators first-round series.

The compliments come for good reason. The 23-year-old added a page to the growing legend of his young career Thursday, leading the team to a 2-1 overtime victory against the Predators.

"Most of the time, the hockey gods are going to reward you for that hard work," Makar said of his team's resolve as it seized a 2-0 series lead. "We were able to get a lucky one in overtime."

The game saw a David turn into a Goliath for Nashville as third-string Predators goalie Connor Ingram became the unlikeliest of near-heroes. Appearing in only his fifth NHL game, he slid across his crease with ease and refused to overplay shots, stymying the Avalanche players no matter what they threw at him. By night's end, he saved 49 shots.

Thanks to Makar, he couldn't make a 50th. After a Nico Sturm shot deflected off Predators captain Roman Josi, Makar seized the puck and fired it on net. Logan O'Connor — a healthy scratch in Game 1 — jumped to let the puck fly toward the net and blocked Ingram's vision in the process. Makar's shot snuck through his legs.

"I think that was the first one all game that I didn't get eyes on before it got to me," Ingram said.

"We get a lucky bounce," Makar added. "I just tried to throw it at the net. Then it was craziness."

He lifted both arms in the air after the puck crossed the line, and Sturm immediately wrapped him in a bear hug, raising a celebratory fist. Josi slammed his fists on his knees in frustration, and Ingram turned around to look into the net. When he saw the puck nestled past the goal line, he lowered his head, defeated.

Back in Makar's hometown of Calgary, his dad, Gary, let out an adrenaline-fueled yell. He later joked that people in Denver probably heard him. He'd tried to do his part from afar, going through various superstitions in attempts to break Ingram's spell.

"I was wearing my Avs jersey inside out, my Avs hat and Avs T-shirt backwards," he said via text.

The goal was a fitting ending to an all-time showing. Makar had 12 shots on the night, a franchise record for a playoff game, and he had another 10 shot attempts blocked. Colorado had 42 shot attempts at five-on-five while he was on the ice, per Natural Stat Trick, while Nashville had only 15. And he played sound defense throughout the night, helping Colorado kill off a five-on-three Nashville power play.

"I thought he was outstanding," coach Jared Bednar said. "I don't know what else to say."

From the beginning of the season, Bednar and his players haven't shied away from saying they believe they have a team capable of winning the Stanley Cup. If they're going to reach that peak, Game 2 is the type of game they'll need to continue to win: one in which players created their own luck and worked for their own breaks.

"Our message was, 'Keep doing what we're doing,'" Bednar said. "You've got to believe that if you keep playing like that and keep doing the right thing and your checking game is in order that you're going to find the way from sheer numbers."

Nathan MacKinnon, Colorado's superstar center, made sure the team got off to a good start. Five minutes into the contest, Erik Johnson chipped a puck out of the defensive zone, and MacKinnon read the play perfectly, seizing possession in stride and galloping up ice. As he neared the net, he lasered a shot to Connor Ingram's right, beating him blocker side to give Colorado a 1-0 lead on the team's first shot of the game. "Let's fucking go," he said to Bowen Byram as the defenseman skated toward him to celebrate.

Over the past three seasons, MacKinnon has played in 27 postseason contests and has 20 goals and 24 assists. He's averaging 1.4 points per game in his playoff career, which is third all-time among players who have appeared in more than 40 postseason games. Only Gretzky (1.84) and Mario Lemieux (1.61) are ahead of him.

"He lives to compete," Makar said. "He's definitely a different animal in the playoffs. That's why he's probably the best player in the world."

But the Predators showed that, unlike in Game 1's 7-2 Colorado victory, an early goal wouldn't lead to a blowout. With just under five minutes left in the first, Josi threw a puck up ice. Samuel Girard crouched in an attempt to stop the puck, but it landed right in front of him and skipped through his legs. His instincts were right, but the result proved costly. Yakov Trenin grabbed possession and flung the puck past Darcy Kuemper, who was playing on his 32nd birthday.

The ice tilted in Colorado's way starting in the second, but the Avalanche couldn't capitalize on three power plays. After getting outshot in the first period, Bednar's club led 43-15 in shots the rest of the game.

"Our forecheck wasn't as effective as it was in Game 1 (in) the first period, and we wanted to make sure we were getting up and turning pucks over and spending some time in the offensive zone," the coach said. "As the game went on, we got better and better at getting to the net and trying to get in his eyes. ... I liked what I saw on the offensive side of it."

At the end of the second period, Valeri Nichushkin seemingly scored a goal, but the referee ruled Artturi Lehkonen interfered with Ingram. Bednar challenged, believing Predators defenseman Dante Fabbro pushed his forward into the goaltender.

But the officials confirmed the call, ruling Leh-konen had "a significant presence in the crease and made incidental contact" with Ingram, according to a statement. They handed Colorado a bench minor penalty for delay of game, so Nashville started the second period on the power play.

Colorado's bad situation quickly got worse, as Nichushkin took a high-sticking penalty almost immediately to start the third period. The Predators all of a sudden had nearly two minutes of five-on-three power-play time. But the Avalanche responded. Darren Helm, Josh Manson and Erik Johnson played the first minute of the kill, frustrating the Predators and clearing the puck. J.T. Compher, Devon Toews and Makar took the ice next, and though Filip Forsberg hit the iron with a shot, the most dangerous chance of Nashville's five-on-three came from Makar. He seized the puck and darted up ice for a partial breakaway. Ingram snared his shot, but Colorado snared momentum.

"They got a few good opportunities, but we were able to weather it," Makar said. "There's not much else to say. We just wanted to gain momentum."

But Ingram made it tough. He halted good Colorado chances on a power play late in the third, and he stood firm the first eight minutes of overtime. All Colorado could do was push and push, and finally Makar broke through. It wasn't his prettiest shot of the night, but it was his most important.

"He does things as a defenseman that offensively a lot of other players can't do," Predators coach John Hynes said. "Because of his quickness, movement and lateral ability, he finds a way to get a lot of shots through. He's an excellent player, that's for sure."

Moments of celebration continued after the players left the ice. Avalanche general manager Joe Sakic rode down the elevator with a smile on his face. Devon Toews signed a jersey for Sawyer Mac-Farland, son of assistant general manager Chris MacFarland, and players' wives and girlfriends cheered whenever one of their partners entered the family room. Kuemper, having made 25 saves on the night, left grinning with his wife.

"We're going to enjoy it and be happy that we got rewarded for all the work we put in tonight, but we know the toughest game is always the next one," the goalie said. "We've got to get ready for that one."

Heading into the playoffs, MacKinnon stressed the importance of the Avalanche's depth, stopping to add one caveat: The team's top players will, in his words, have to "drive the bus" if Colorado is going to make a deep run.

That sentiment rang true Thursday, and it was Makar's turn to grab the wheel. ▬▬

'He Was Everywhere'

Avalanche's Cale Makar Finishes Off a Dominant Series

By Peter Baugh

MAY 10, 2022

Cale Makar doesn't always make sense. How is someone so soft-spoken, humble and polite so ruthless when on skates?

"He might be the best player in the league right now," teammate Nathan MacKinnon said after Colorado's 5-3 win Monday to clinch a first-round series win against the Predators.

With the score tied at 3-3 and Nashville clinging to its last shreds of hope midway through the third, Makar turned into a heartbreaker, escaping from Yakov Trenin along the boards and darting toward the net. Predators defenseman Dante Fabbro skated to help stop Makar, and goalie Connor Ingram shifted over to face his opponent, too. Why wouldn't he? The 23-year-old Avalanche star had haunted Nashville skaters and goalies all series.

But Makar's skating isn't the only elite part of his game. His vision is, too. He knew the Predators had played primarily in a man-to-man structure, so he figured someone would be open near the net once he beat Trenin. Sure enough, Valeri Nichushkin was waiting, and Makar zipped him a pass. The Russian winger slammed it into the vacated portion of the net.

"Great play by Val to find that space," MacKinnon said. "Great play all around."

And Makar's pass was a fitting coup de grace for a series he dominated.

"He was everywhere," coach Jared Bednar said.

Makar's dominance flummoxed the Predators players and frustrated their fans, so much so that they threw candy at Makar with a minute left in the game.

"Obviously, not a fun way for your team to end the season like that, but a couple Skittles were hitting me during the play," said Makar, who was less than pleased but praised the Nashville atmosphere up to that point.

The win sent Colorado to the second round for the fourth consecutive year, and Bednar's club will look to get over the hump and make it to the conference finals or beyond. The Avalanche should have almost all players available for the series, assuming Andrew Cogliano and Ryan Murray are cleared by Game 1. Starting goaltender Darcy Kuemper is recovering from a stick blade to the face, but he would have been able to play Monday if the swelling near his eye had gone down. Pavel Francouz played in his place, stopping 28 of 31 shots.

"I thought he was good," Bednar said. "We had a couple bad line changes that led to odd-man rushes. They scored two goals on poor line changes from us — mental mistakes from us. But Frankie, I thought he looked pretty good tonight. ... Comes in tonight, finishes the job. Good on him."

Though Nashville showed fight throughout the night, the Avalanche jumped to a lead early — and in a bizarre fashion. Less than two minutes into the game, Andre Burakovsky flung the puck past Ingram, and it tore through the top of the net, bouncing out the back. Burakovsky and Bowen Byram, who assisted on the play, started to celebrate, but play continued with the puck bouncing around.

Meanwhile, on the Avalanche bench, video coach Brett Heimlich pulled up a replay and tried to alert the officials. Finally, at the next stoppage, around 45 seconds later, the play was reviewed. Sure enough, it was a good, twine-snapping goal.

Net-tearing goals aren't common, but they're also not unheard of. Team Canada's Shea Weber blasted a slap shot through the net at the 2010 Olympics. It happens "more than you'd think," Bednar said.

But the fact that Burakovsky managed to sever the twine with a wrister was impressive, nonetheless.

"He's got a heavy shot," MacKinnon said.

Burakovsky, whom Bednar has described as a streaky scorer, hadn't logged a point in the playoffs before the goal, though he was strong defensively in Round 1. He finished the night with three points after a pair of assists in the third period.

"You're hoping it's going to carry over (to the second round)," Bednar said. "There's been a heightened determination in his game in the playoffs so far. ... He was a huge difference-maker for us tonight. Hopefully, he can get some confidence from that."

Avalanche captain Gabriel Landeskog said going into the game that he expected the Predators to play hard and try to avoid a sweep on home ice. Sure enough, they responded to Burakovsky's goal. Late in the first, Nico Sturm couldn't get the puck out of the defensive zone, and Colton Sissons snatched it, passing to Trenin in the slot. The winger zinged a shot past Francouz to tie the score.

The Predators sustained pressure on the Avalanche to start the second, but Colorado still managed to limit them to seven total shots through the first 30 minutes. And with 7:46 left, Francouz made a nifty glove save, snagging an Eeli Tolvanen laser to keep the score at 1-1. Less than two minutes later, Makar decided he was tired of the tie. He beat Ingram with a wrister from the point, placing the puck perfectly in the top left corner of the net. The goal was his third of the series, and he ultimately finished with seven assists. His 10 points are the most in NHL history by a defenseman in four games to start the playoffs, according to the league.

"The way he dominates from the back end is amazing," MacKinnon said. "He might be one of the best D to ever play by the end of his career."

The blueliner nearly scored moments after his second-period goal, grabbing the puck on a breakaway and getting a shot on net, but Ingram stood firm to keep the Predators within one. The save loomed large later in the second. With a little more than three minutes left in the period, Francouz halted Sissons on a breakaway, but the puck bounced to Trenin, who potted it from the faceoff circle for his second tally. The Avalanche nearly snatched the lead back with a minute left in the period.

As the third period began, Nashville hadn't led all series, but that changed four minutes into the period. Mattias Ekholm found Filip Forsberg, who waited at the back door for an easy tap-in.

"Definitely a kick in the ass," Makar said. "Excuse my language."

MacKinnon said the deficit was a good challenge, and Devon Toews fired in a shot midway through the frame to tie the score. That preceded Makar's wizardry and Nichushkin's go-ahead tally, and MacKinnon iced the game with an empty-net tally. He blew a goodbye kiss to the Nashville crowd.

"They had a good game tonight; I felt like we didn't have a great one," MacKinnon said. "That's going to happen eventually, but we found a way. That's the key."

Back in March, Calgary coach Darryl Sutter said playing Colorado in the first round would be "a waste of eight days" for a wild-card team. For the Predators, who got a full dose of MacKinnon and Makar and the Avalanche offense, Sutter's words proved prophetic. ▬▬

Josh Manson

Snowboard Dreams, a Lucic Fight and a Lucky Haircut

By Peter Baugh

MAY 19, 2022

Josh Manson wanted to quit hockey. He had never felt much passion playing the sport and, as a 12-year-old in Prince Albert, Saskatchewan, wasn't sure he'd like the coach on the team he was set to join. Snowboarding, meanwhile, was fun. There weren't mountains near his home, but he loved taking his board to a local hill and flying down the slope. That's how he wanted to spend his free time, he decided.

So as the start of the hockey season approached, Manson approached his mom, Lana, and told her he thought he was done with it. Manson's parents never forced the sport on him, despite the fact that his dad, Dave, played more than 1,100 NHL games, but in this instance, Lana put her foot down. She didn't want her son to quit a sport before even giving his new team and new coach a chance.

"No chance, buddy," Manson remembers her saying. "You've got to see this thing through."

Good move, Mom.

Manson says that was the year hockey grasped him. He loved his coach. He loved putting in the effort needed to maximize his potential. He loved helping the team, and he believes the experience helped him find himself.

"It could have come to an abrupt halt when I was 12 years old," Manson says. "Thank goodness my mom stepped in."

"It was just a good experience overall," Lana adds. "He was playing well and had good people to be with. That just made him a little more passionate."

The Avalanche are current benefactors of Lana's insistence. Ahead of the trade deadline, Colorado general manager Joe Sakic saw Manson as a necessary addition to a roster with Stanley Cup aspirations, acquiring the defenseman from Anaheim for prospect Drew Helleson and a second-round pick. The move looked genius in Game 1 of the second round Tuesday as Manson potted an overtime winner past a seemingly impenetrable Jordan Binnington in St. Louis' net. He leaped into the air after he saw the puck cross the goal line, throwing his arms above his head.

"It's been fun to watch," says Lana, who watched from her couch in Edmonton and also threw her hands up after the goal. "Especially when Josh has that big smile."

Playing as well as he has since joining the Avalanche, Manson is as far as could be from his snowboarding days. Now when he sees the mountains in Denver, he doesn't think about his former passion. That itch has passed; he hasn't gotten on a board for more than a decade.

"I'm a hockey player now," he says.

A little more than a decade ago, Manson wasn't much of an NHL prospect. Heck, he wasn't even a full-time defenseman.

Back in his developmental years, Manson almost exclusively played forward. The now-30-year-old didn't switch positions until his second year with the Salmon Arm Silverbacks, a Junior A team in the British Columbia Hockey League.

"Even by his own opinion, he was someone who was a little bit of a late bloomer," says Cam Fowler, his former teammate with the Ducks.

Manson's first year with the Silverbacks started right around his 18th birthday, and he struck up a friendship with linemate Devin Gannon. They played video games together, watched sports and spent time on the golf course, where Gannon remembers being awed by his buddy's strength when he drove the green on a par 4. Manson also would pull out his guitar to play, and Gannon says he has a good singing voice.

Early in Manson's second season with Salmon Arm, his coach, Tim Kehler, suggested he try out defense. Another player the coach had worked with had benefited from a position change, and he thought Manson could be similar.

At first, Manson felt like he was struggling. The move didn't seem to work, so he switched back to forward. But later in the season, when the team was without multiple defensemen, Manson played out of necessity. That's when things began to shift.

"It went well," he says. "I kind of found my way through it."

He ended the year with 47 points in 57 games, up from 24 points the year before. And at least one NHL team took notice: Anaheim picked him that summer in the sixth round of the 2011 draft. Though he had yet to play a full season at defense, the switch was already paying dividends.

"Josh has always been a simple player," Gannon says. "You're not going to see many toe-drags, but he always makes the smart play. That translated right to D where he was making that first pass out of the zone. His mistakes were limited. It was just a very easy transition for him. I'm sure he'll tell you differently, but he made it look pretty easy."

Not everyone can fight Milan Lucic. The bruising 6-foot-4 forward is viewed as one of the tougher players in the league, and he's never afraid to drop the gloves.

Neither, Anaheim quickly learned, is Manson. Back in the 2015 preseason, after a three-year NCAA career at Northeastern and with only 28 NHL games to his name, Manson objected to a Lucic — then with the rival Kings — hit on Chris Wagner, and the two immediately squared off. Their bout lasted a full minute and ended with Lucic bringing him to the ice. That didn't matter to the Ducks bench. The full team applauded by tapping their sticks against the boards, a memory that still jumps out to Fowler.

"I remember watching it from the bench and being blown away by the toughness he showed and the willingness to get in there," says Fowler, at that point a five-year veteran. "It kind of set the tone for what he was willing to do for our team and what he continued to do up until the day he ended up going somewhere else."

Gannon remembers Manson's willingness to fight in the BCHL, too. Off the ice, he was "a very kind individual," his former teammate says, but if he didn't like a hit on a teammate, he'd never shy away from a fight. His Ducks teammates took to him quickly, and he lived with Andrew Cogliano — who is also now with the Avalanche — as he got settled in the NHL. Cogliano says he made Manson drive him "everywhere" and calls him "one of the best guys I've met in the game."

On the ice, Manson brought his team more than just toughness and a 6-foot-3 frame. Fowler noticed his poise immediately, and he earned a reputation for strong defense. Manson helped the Ducks to the conference finals in 2017, and he ended up playing 22 career postseason games for the club.

"He's the type of guy that other players in the league don't enjoy playing against, because he plays hard, he's physical and he makes you earn it," Cogliano says. "He's a presence."

The Ducks failed to make the playoffs after 2018, and with the team in a rebuilding phase and Manson's contract set to expire this offseason, the team began shopping him ahead of the March trade deadline.

For the Avalanche, who needed another defenseman and struggled against a physical Vegas team in the 2021 playoffs, Manson emerged as a fit. The trade went through March 14, an off day in New York for the Ducks. As Fowler left the team hotel for dinner, a fan seeking autographs told him the news: His primary D partner in 2021-22 was on the move.

"We've both grown up in this organization," Fowler says. "It hit me a little harder when he was moved. But he's got a great opportunity now with a great team."

Adds Lana Manson: "He was really lucky to go to Colorado."

After finalizing the deal for Manson, Sakic came down to coach Jared Bednar's office to tell him the news. The coach was instantly excited. This wasn't a young player or Eastern Conference transplant he needed to do film study on. Bednar immediately knew what the defenseman could bring.

"It was the type of guy we'd probably been missing," the coach says. "They're hard to find. Teams generally don't move guys of his caliber."

But as happy as the Avalanche might have been to make the move, the on-ice transition wasn't seamless. Manson had been with the Ducks for

450-plus games, and he had to adjust to a new structure. He was thinking too much on the ice, Bednar says, and the defenseman said late in the regular season that he needed to let the game come to him. During a four-game Colorado skid less than two weeks before the playoffs began, Manson had a minus-5 rating and took two minor penalties. All of the sudden, his play looked like a reason for concern, not excitement.

Manson cut his hair ahead of an April 26 game against St. Louis, ditching his shoulder-length locks. After scoring against the Blues that night, he joked that his goal had "everything" to do with his fresh haircut. And whether it's because of the haircut (unlikely) or more comfort in the Colorado systems (more likely), Manson's game turned a corner in the final three regular-season games and in Colorado's first-round series with Nashville. He's fit into a second-pairing role where he helps create space for partner Samuel Girard, a strong skater with a smaller frame. He finished with the second-highest Game Score (4.32) in the league Tuesday night, according to Hockey Stat Cards, trailing only his partner, Girard (4.39).

"As he's gotten more clear on (the structure), he's become more dangerous offensively, he's become a better defender for us and a really relied-upon guy," Bednar says. "Now we're seeing exactly why we did get him."

If all goes well for the Manson family, the conference finals could serve as a reunion. Dave Manson is an assistant with the Oilers, who are playing the Flames in a second-round series, so if both Edmonton and Colorado win their series, the father and son will face off. Manson talked to his dad after the Oilers beat Los Angeles in Game 7 of the first round, and Lana says Dave told their son, "We're coming for you!" The two have a close relationship, and Josh told TNT after his overtime winner that Dave passed along a few tips on the Blues.

"He's been amazing with that throughout my entire life, just being able to compartmentalize things for me and be a hockey dad when he needs to be a hockey dad and be just dad when he needs to be dad," Manson says.

According to Manson and those around him, he has enjoyed his time in Denver, though he says he hasn't thought much about the prospect of signing beyond this year. For now, that's out of his control.

How he plays, on the other hand, is in his control, and he's enjoyed the feeling of being on a winning team.

"It's a different mentality," he told reporters shortly after the trade. "You can feel it: Guys in the room expect to win. It's intoxicating. You feel it and you're like, 'Let's keep winning. This is fun.'" ▬▬

The Villain

Avalanche's Nazem Kadri Embraces Road Role with Game 4 Hat Trick

By Peter Baugh

MAY 24, 2022

Nazem Kadri stared down middle fingers. He silenced the booing crowd. He celebrated. He shoved.

And, most problematically for his opponents, he scored. Quite a bit.

"I think he liked being the villain tonight," teammate Erik Johnson said after the Avalanche's 6-3 Game 4 win against the Blues on Monday. "He certainly stepped up for us."

Kadri said after the game that the past two days have been upsetting. In Game 3 on Saturday, he and St. Louis defenseman Calle Rosen collided with Blues goalie Jordan Binnington, leaving the St. Louis netminder injured. In the injury's aftermath, Kadri received threatening and Islamophobic messages, and the Avalanche released a statement Sunday saying they were working with local law enforcement to investigate. TSN's Darren Dreger reported the police enhanced security procedures at both the team hotel and the arena.

"I know what was said isn't a reflection on every single fan in St. Louis. I understand that and I want to make that clear," Kadri said. "But for those that wasted their time sending messages like that, I feel sorry for them."

He said the situation only gave him fuel. And he had exactly the impact the Blues didn't want, registering a hat trick and getting under their skin throughout the game.

"I just want to say how proud we are of Naz to go through all that crap the last couple days," said Johnson, who added a tally of his own Monday. "No person should have to go through that. He sure responded."

After falling behind 1-0 in the first period of Game 4, Colorado came out with the buzz of a wasp's nest in the second frame, perhaps with some subliminal help from the Blues organist, who played a rendition of Blink-182's song "All The Small Things." At Avalanche games in Denver, the jam serves as a third-period anthem when Colorado is holding on to a lead. And, as if by Pavlovian response, the Avalanche players solved goalie Ville Husso, who had held them scoreless in the first. Johnson scored the equalizer, and it took less than two minutes for the Avalanche to score again, marking the beginning of Kadri's involvement on the scoresheet.

With 16 minutes left in the frame, Valeri Nichushkin found Kadri with a long pass, setting up a two-on-one rush. Kadri glanced at teammate Mikko Rantanen, who had joined him on the break, but opted to shoot himself, tucking the puck just under Husso's glove.

The Avalanche center, who has been booed every time he's touched the puck since Binnington's injury, held his hand to his ear, and his message was clear: I can't hear you now.

"I appreciate (the boos)," Kadri said. "I like when fans are engaged in the game and have something to cheer about. If you want to boo, by all means. That doesn't bother me at all."

Quite the opposite, it appears. He feeds off it. Devon Toews scored, and with the Avalanche up 3-1, Kadri aggravated Blues forward David Perron, bumping him after a whistle. St. Louis forward Pavel Buchnevich responded by shoving Kadri to the ice, and as Kadri started standing up, Perron threw him back to the ice, then dove on top of him.

The result: Perron and Buchnevich sat in the penalty box, and Colorado got a five-on-three power play.

"That's just stupid penalties that we cashed in on, and it hurt them," Kadri said. "If you lose your cool, we'll make you pay."

Added Johnson: "We're just going to stay out of that stuff. We're going to look the other way. It's not about ego; it's about winning."

Sure enough, Colorado capitalized on the two-man advantage. Though the Avalanche didn't technically score while Perron and Buchnevich were in the box, they generated a scoring chance right as the power play expired. Rookie Bowen Byram, who took on added responsibility with Samuel Girard hurt, passed to Kadri, and the veteran potted his second of the night. In fewer than five minutes, the explosive Colorado offense had scored four goals.

As Kadri turned to celebrate, Perron tried to elbow him up high, but he avoided the contact then stared right into the faces of two Blues fans flipping him off. He bathed in their jeers.

"I think (the middle fingers) came after the celly," Kadri said. "But hey, I've got to rub it in."

And he continued to do so with his play. The Blues came back, cutting the Avalanche lead to 4-3 with a pair of power-play goals and setting up higher stakes for Kadri's third tally of the night.

With 10 minutes left in the game, Nichushkin nudged a puck away from Jordan Kyrou, and it bounced to Kadri, charging into the slot. He snatched the puck from the ice and flung a wrist shot at Husso's net. The goalie couldn't manage to stop it with his stick, and Kadri unleashed his third and final post-goal celebration of the night, dropping to a knee and punching the air.

"I wanted to come out tonight and really put a mark on this game, especially after what happened," he said. "I was able to strike early in the second period and was able to get the mojo going, in terms of individually and as a team. So it felt amazing. Especially to do it on the road. It was pure."

Kadri has four goals and two assists in the past two games, and all six of his points came after the St. Louis fans started booing every time he touched the puck. He chipped in a final point Monday, assisting Rantanen's empty-netter to put the score at 6-3.

After the game, Bednar said the team moved past the threats toward Kadri and focused on winning. But the coach acknowledged the center himself might have a tougher time focusing than others, considering the threats and messages were directed at him.

"He proved tonight that he's able to do that," Bednar said. "He knows we're all with him."

Kadri showing up under bright lights shouldn't have come as a surprise. He always has to raise the stakes with bets while golfing with friends, childhood buddy Jason McNeill said earlier this season, and his wife, Ashley, has seen how intense he gets playing pickup basketball with his dad and cousins. He even hates to lose in putt-putt, she says.

"Obviously a tremendous game from him," Bednar said. "I'm really proud of the way he's handled the last 48 hours, and to be able to come out and perform like that in the pressure situation is amazing."

Kadri took motivation from more than just the threats and hateful messages. He didn't like hearing when Craig Berube said, "Look at (Kadri's) reputation" in response to a question about Kadri's role in the Binnington collision. The Avalanche center, of course, served an eight-game suspension last postseason for a high hit on Blues defenseman Justin Faulk, and the league

suspended him twice in the playoffs while he was with Toronto.

"(Berube) made some comments that I wasn't a fan of," said Kadri, who insists he was going for the loose puck in front of Binnington's crease. "I guess he's never heard of bulletin-board material."

He used it to his advantage Monday, and now the Avalanche have a chance to conquer the Blues and their second-round demons when they play Wednesday.

Game 3, with the Binnington collision and go-ahead goal, will likely go down in St. Louis — and perhaps Denver — as the Nazem Kadri Game.

Well, sequels don't always live up to originals. But in front of a building filled with boos Monday, Kadri made sure that wasn't the case this time. ▬▬

Getting Over the Hump

Avalanche Finally Break Through Second Round Thanks to Darren Helm, J.T. Compher

By Peter Baugh

MAY 28, 2022

Darren Helm. Career grinder. Longtime Red Wing. Veteran penalty killer. And now, certifiably and undeniably, a scorer of big goals.

Detroit fans know it well. In 2009, Helm potted an overtime winner to beat an emerging Chicago club and send the Red Wings to the Stanley Cup Final. He was only 22 back then, a late-round draft pick making an impact on the tail end of a Detroit dynasty.

More than a decade and one uniform change later, Helm tallied a series-winning goal once again, this time sending the Avalanche to the Western Conference final with a 3-2 win against the Blues. The goal came on May 27, 2022, 13 years to the day after his overtime winner with the Red Wings.

"What a day for you," teammate Josh Manson said while sitting next to him in their postgame news conference.

"My mom's birthday is tomorrow, too," Helm responded. "Happy birthday, Mom!"

He gave her quite a present.

With seven seconds left and the score tied 2-2, Logan O'Connor fired the puck across the ice in the Avalanche offensive zone. It bounced off the boards and right to Helm. He saw the pass coming, and his thoughts echoed those of his coach on the Avalanche bench.

"I was saying to myself, 'Shoot it,'" Jared Bednar said. "'Just shoot it.'"

And Helm did. He wound up for a slap shot from the faceoff circle and propelled the puck forward. It zinged over Blues forward Alexei Toropchenko's leg. It sailed past Gabriel Landeskog's outstretched stick. It continued to the left of goalie Ville Husso's glove. And finally, with 5.6 seconds left on the clock, it struck the mesh netting. The Avalanche had the lead.

Helm circled toward the glass, crouching in elation and letting out a scream. O'Connor reached him first and jumped into his arms. Nathan MacKinnon leaped up and down on the bench. Manson had his head down, praying. He missed seeing the goal go in, but it was impossible not to notice his elated teammates celebrating all around him. He instantly joined in.

"Just the best feeling," Manson said. "Almost relief. You're so excited, but it's like, 'Thank goodness, it's over, we did it. We got the job done.' That was one of the highs in my hockey career."

Goalie Darcy Kuemper had to make one final save on a long-distance shot from Justin Faulk, and he shoveled the puck to the side of the net so time could expire. And with that, the Avalanche are off to the Western Conference final for the first time in a decade. They'll host the Edmonton Oilers for Game 1 on Tuesday.

"From the drop of the puck tonight, you could tell that we were ready to go," Bednar said. "You could tell the belief was there."

And Helm, one of only two players in the Avalanche lineup Friday who has a Stanley Cup ring, was the one to make it happen. General manager Joe Sakic signed him last offseason to a one-year deal — an unheralded transaction at the time — and the forward had an up-and-down season, dealing with injuries and producing only 15 points in 68 games. He had the second-lowest plus-minus rating on the team (minus-5) and at points late in the season was a healthy scratch.

But he's found his groove in the playoffs, helping create an effective fourth line with O'Connor, Andrew Cogliano and, at points, Nico Sturm.

"They're maybe not going to be as pretty or fancy to watch as say MacKinnon's line, but they had an impact on the game," Bednar said of the fourth line's play in Game 6. "And then Helm ends up getting a really huge goal for our organization." "There's no other guy who deserves it more than he does," said Landeskog, the team captain.

The former Red Wing is the type of player needed to win a championship, Detroit legend Pavel Datsyuk told The Athletic earlier this year. Helm is a hard worker, said legendary defenseman Nicklas Lidstrom, Helm's first captain with the Red Wings, who noted his relentlessness on the puck.

"Just a hard guy to play against," Lidstrom said.

Added Darren McCarty, another former Detroit teammate, "Helmer's a great example (of) being a veteran guy that you can get at a good price that has everything you need to go in that locker room because of not only his experience but of who he is and the role that he plays."

Players like Helm were the ones Colorado needed against a tenacious Blues team in Game 6. The team's stars generated chances — MacKinnon, Landeskog, Mikko Rantanen and Cale Makar all had an Expected Goals For rate above 70 percent, per Natural Stat Trick — but the bottom-six forward group, which had combined for only one goal in the first five games of the series, provided all the team's scoring.

"If we're going to win, we need everybody," MacKinnon said. "I know it's a cliché, but you look at any team that wins, everybody's chipping in, and that's kind of been our team this year in the playoffs."

First came J.T. Compher. With the Avalanche down a goal in the second period, he snatched a rebound off a Manson shot and batted it past Husso. Andre Burakovsky, a healthy scratch the previous two games, logged a secondary assist on the play – his 13th point in his past nine potential close-out playoff games. The tie was short-lived, though, as Blues forward Brayden Schenn capitalized on a Jack Johnson fumble at the blue line and led a two-on-one break. He passed to Jordan Kyrou, who beat Kuemper to make it 2-1.

"There was no frustration on the bench," Compher said. "We kept rolling them over, keeping the pressure on. The main thing was the belief. We kept believing we'd get the job done."

And Manson stepped up with a big defensive play to make sure that had a chance of happening. During a Blues power play in the second period, Kyrou got the puck in front of the Avalanche net and deked out Kuemper with a delayed shot. The netminder found himself sprawling out of his crease, so Kyrou kept moving toward the front of the net, looking for an angle to shoot. He found a lane to whip in a backhander, but as he let the puck go, Manson planted himself in the crease. The puck hit his chest and trickled to Kuemper, who covered it.

"There was a bit of a panic, to be honest with you," Manson said. "Once it went to Kyrou, I knew he was really a patient player, and I had a feeling he was gonna hold on to that thing. Once I saw him take the step, I just was hoping that it (would) hit me."

That kept the Avalanche within a goal of St. Louis, and Compher put on his superhero cape once again in the second, wristing a shot past Husso as the Avalanche power play expired. As Bednar said postgame, Compher had himself a night.

"I wanted him to be more assertive and not so safe," the coach said, and he got what he wanted.

According to Natural Stat Trick, Colorado led the Blues in scoring chances (35-17), high-danger chances (15-5) and expected goals (3.21-1.49). And finally, that culminated in a lead with Helm's goal just ahead of the buzzer.

After the game, Blues players walked toward the Avalanche dressing room to congratulate their adversaries. Schenn chatted with MacKinnon, and Nick Leddy and Brandon Saad said hello to Devon Toews and Johnson. All three of those St. Louis players have their names on the Stanley Cup.

"They're a good team, no doubt about it," Schenn said in his postgame news conference.

Bednar said earlier in the series that the Avalanche weren't focused on beating Round 2. They were focused on beating St. Louis. But getting over the second-round hump is enormous for the organization, regardless of whether it has bigger goals or not. Colorado hasn't been in the conference finals since the 2001-02 season. Bowen Byram, the youngest player on the Avalanche roster, was less than a year old at the time. Bednar was still playing pro hockey, and the Colorado roster featured five of the organization's six players with retired numbers.

"Obviously, the job's not finished," MacKinnon said. "But that's a great accomplishment for us."

But recent history, not events of 20 years ago, is what makes the achievement sweet. The Avalanche have been building to this point, but the second round has marked a stumbling block, like a glitch that doesn't let you go past a certain point in a video game. In 2019, they lost by a goal to San Jose in Game 7, in which the game-tying Colin Wilson goal was overturned in a controversial offside decision. The next year, an injury-riddled team on its third-string goaltender couldn't hold on to a one-goal lead late in Game 7, losing to the Stars in overtime.

And then came last summer's Vegas series, which saw Colorado hop out to a 2-0 lead and implode. That's the series Bednar said hurt most. It wasn't inexperience or injuries that cost the Avalanche. It was their own play.

"Those are lessons," the coach said. "You have to go through them, and you have to go through the heartbreak. I feel we're better off for it."

Against the Golden Knights, Colorado crumbled after blowing a late lead in Game 3. When the Avs got their game back, it was too late to salvage the series.

Players on this year's team stressed their increased maturity, their growth. But those words could only mean so much until the Avalanche backed them up. And after a draining overtime loss in Game 5 in which they blew a three-goal lead, that's exactly what they did, thanks to a third-period comeback and a last-second shot from a veteran who'd been in big moments before. ▬▬

Nathan MacKinnon

Avalanche Star Showing His Maturity, Embracing Playoff Journey

By Peter Baugh

MAY 29, 2022

Nathan MacKinnon had only known the losing end of the second round.

Last year, he fired a slapper on Vegas' net as the clock expired in Game 6, as if shooting hard enough could account for the three goals needed to tie the game. The postseason before, he stared blankly from the bench as Dallas' players celebrated their Game 7 overtime win. And in 2019, he walked through the handshake line, stopping to congratulate goalie Martin Jones on handing Colorado a one-goal loss in Game 7.

The Avalanche star didn't want any of that to happen again, especially knowing the talent on Colorado's roster. So he did all he could to ensure an Avalanche victory in Game 5, completing a hat trick with an all-time, coast-to-coast goal Wednesday. But it wasn't enough, as St. Louis scored a score-tying goal in the final minute and won in overtime.

"Hopefully everything happens for a reason," he said after that game. "We've got to go get this done."

This is a man who hates losing. As far back as when he was at Shattuck-St. Mary's, a prep high school in Minnesota, he and friend Danny Tirone wouldn't talk to each other for hours after contentious pingpong battles, Tirone told The Athletic. The two also held a knee hockey tournament in their dorm, using their artistic skills to build a trophy, but when their team lost, they had to leave the room to cool down. Late in one 2019 Avalanche defeat, MacKinnon lost his composure on the bench, spiking his green Gatorade water bottle and snapping at coach Jared Bednar.

Now 26, MacKinnon has emerged as a more mature version of himself. His competitive fire is still ever-present, but over the past few years, he's poured resources into nutrition, fitness and a sports psychologist. So though he was disappointed, naturally, after Game 5, he spoke with more measured tones than in years past. He kept his focus squarely on the future, on what he still believed he and his teammates could accomplish.

And the Avalanche lived up to those words, coming back in the third period Friday to win 3-2 against the Blues and sending MacKinnon to his first Western Conference final. And though the star player didn't dominate the stat sheet, his underlying numbers were excellent. The Avalanche had 81.65 percent of the five-on-five expected goal share with him on the ice in a Game 6 victory, per Natural Stat Trick, and had 11 scoring chances while allowing only three.

"That's Playoff Nate," Cale Makar said of MacKinnon's Game 5 performance, but his words applied to his teammate in Game 6, too. "We don't expect anything less."

MacKinnon went almost exclusively against Ryan O'Reilly in the second round. The Blues captain and former Avalanche player is one of the top defensive forwards in the league, and he won the Conn Smythe and Selke trophies in 2019. And though MacKinnon's point production was lower against St. Louis than previous rounds, he still finished with seven points in the six-game series.

O'Reilly and MacKinnon played more than 80 minutes against each other at five-on-five in the series. The Blues had an edge in goals (4-3) during those minutes, but Colorado dominated possession and shots, helping wear down the Blues' goaltending and defense. The Avalanche had 66.86 percent of the five-on-five expected goals share when MacKinnon and O'Reilly shared the ice, out-chanced the Blues 43-22 and out-high-danger-chanced them 19-11. MacKinnon said going into the series that "the best defense is a good offense, patient offense," and that's what he provided.

MacKinnon, the third-longest-tenured Avalanche player, lived up to his billing as the face of the franchise, showing he can dominate when the moment is most intense. He's a No. 1 pick who has blossomed into an NHL superstar, and now he'll get to play on a bigger stage than he reached in his first eight years.

"It means a lot," he said after the Avalanche's win against the Blues on Friday. "There have been some dark times. Nice to get over this hump, for sure."

Dark times indeed. After a trip to the playoffs in 2013-14, his rookie year, MacKinnon didn't make it back to the postseason until 2017-18. The three seasons in between featured a dismal 2016-17 in which Colorado finished with a league-worst 48 points. The next closest team, Vancouver, had 69.

But the Avalanche progressed under Bednar, ultimately becoming a Stanley Cup threat. They just couldn't get over that pesky second-round hump. Pressure reached a high point this year. Earlier in the season, during an ESPN broadcast, between-the-benches reporter Emily Kaplan said a Vegas player yelled at the Colorado bench, "Get out of the second round, why don't you?" Then general manager Joe Sakic went all-in at the trade deadline, adding the likes of Artturi Lehkonen and Josh Manson.

"I know how much our players want (to win)," Bednar said. "I've been with a lot of these guys now for six years and some of them were here before me, and I've had discussions with them. Even the new guys that we've brought in, trying to win, it's hard. It's really hard."

Because of the degree of difficulty in the playoffs, MacKinnon stressed enjoying the journey. He sure did late in the deciding Game 6 against St. Louis. He was the first player to raise his arms after Darren Helm shot in the winner, quickly joining in a mass of celebrating teammates. And when the final horn blew, he skated straight toward Darcy Kuemper, leaping into his arms in front of the Avalanche net.

"There will only be four teams soon, and obviously the job's not finished, but that's a great accomplishment for us," he said. "I thought we outplayed them for the majority of the series and definitely tonight. We deserved a good bounce there at the end."

Perhaps it would've been sexier if MacKinnon's highlight-reel goal in Game 5 proved to be the series-winner. But MacKinnon is happiest when he wins, regardless of how victory comes about. And that's what the Avalanche did. ▬▬

Taking Control

Nazem Kadri, Avalanche Second Line Dominate in Game 2 Win

By Peter Baugh

JUNE 3, 2022

T he Oilers have the best forward in this series. Avalanche superstar Nathan MacKinnon knows it. He has called Connor McDavid the No. 1 player in the world on multiple occasions. But through two games, Colorado has had an advantage that's too much for one player to match. Even a generational one paired with another former MVP in Leon Draisaitl.

The advantage starts with Nazem Kadri, who can anchor a second line that plays like a first. But it doesn't end there. Colorado has wing depth that, at times, is flat-out overwhelming. That gives coach Jared Bednar options. If he wants to split up Colorado's three top forwards — MacKinnon, Gabriel Landeskog and Mikko Rantanen — he can do so without breaking a sweat, as he's shown throughout the playoffs. And in a 4-0 Game 2 win Thursday against the Oilers, it played out beautifully for the Avalanche, who have a 2-0 series lead.

"(Depth) has been the story all year," Kadri said, mentioning how the team battled through injuries during the season to have the Western Conference's leading record. "We all know playoff hockey. Once it gets to four or two teams, that's going to be a difference-maker, for sure."

Bednar primarily played his top line of Landeskog, MacKinnon and Valeri Nichushkin against McDavid, and the trio did its job of successfully neutralizing the Oilers captain and his linemates. That helped put Kadri, Rantanen and Artturi Lehkonen in position to break through, which they did in the second period.

The line's eruption started when, after a Kadri dump-in, Lehkonen pressured Darnell Nurse in the Avalanche's offensive zone, forcing the defenseman to make an errant pass. Rantanen snatched the puck and got it to Kadri, who fired on net. Lehkonen tipped the shot past goalie Mike Smith and punched the air with excitement.

"Real intelligent player," Bednar said of Lehkonen. "He understands where the other guys are on the ice. He makes a lot of plays that lead to scoring chances."

The line continued to work. Moments after the Avalanche got on the board, a forecheck led by Lehkonen and Rantanen got the puck loose in the offensive zone. Kadri wound up with it on his stick once again and fed Josh Manson, who propelled an 86-mph slap shot past Smith from the slot. Only 15 seconds had passed since Colorado's opening goal, and the second line needed less than two minutes to score again, this time with Edmonton's top line of McDavid, Evander Kane and Zach Hyman on the ice. Kadri seized the puck from Kane in the defensive zone, then sped past him to create a two-on-one rush with Rantanen. Once in the offensive zone, he got the puck under Nurse's stick to his winger, and Rantanen finished.

With that, the Avalanche led 3-0, and all of their goals came with primary helpers from Kadri.

"That line has seemed to find some chemistry," the center said. "We're going to look to keep it up."

Added Bednar, "That's the line that got us started and kept it going in the second period."

Rantanen's scoring surge is particularly encouraging for Colorado. He had only one playoff goal entering the series, and that was an empty-net tally. Now he has two in as many games in the Western Conference final, which has marked the first time he has consistently played with Kadri and Lehkonen during these playoffs.

"Mikko is too good to not get on the scoresheet," Kadri said. "He's got a great shot, he's a big body, hockey IQ is off the charts. It was only a matter of time for him, the way he can distribute, too. He doesn't have to score and facilitate and make other players better. He's catching fire at the right time."

The Lehkonen-Kadri-Rantanen line had 86.04 percent of the expected goal share at five-on-five, according to Natural Stat Trick, which led all Avalanche line combinations that played more than six minutes together. They generated 10 scoring chances together, by far the most on the team, while allowing only two.

Bednar tried different combinations late in the regular season in hopes of building chemistry among different groupings of players. That's paying off big time in the playoffs, as he has frequently jumbled his top-six wingers around centers MacKinnon and Kadri. Landeskog, Nichushkin, Lehkonen and Rantanen have all spent time on the top and second lines this postseason.

The depth doesn't stop with the top-six forwards, though. The bottom two lines have contributed, too, even if their numbers aren't as noticeable. Andrew Cogliano, Darren Helm and Logan O'Connor have found an identity as a fourth line, and they weren't on the ice for a five-on-five scoring chance against Thursday. And though the third line had a quiet night in Game 2, J.T. Compher had two goals in the opener against Edmonton and in Game 6 against St. Louis.

"Everyone contributes, and it's definitely tough to keep up with," Kadri said.

It was more than enough support Thursday for Pavel Francouz, who started in net with Darcy Kuemper out and day to day with an upper-body injury. The Czech netminder kept the Oilers off the board, posting a 24-save shutout and ending nine-game point streaks for Draisaitl and McDavid. He stymied Kane in front of the net minutes into the game and helped stop two Oilers power plays before the night was done.

"I thought he was great," Bednar said. "Looked poised, calm, really confident."

Fans showered him with, "Frankie! Frankie! Frankie!" chants that continued as they exited the building. With Colorado in need of a steady goalie showing, he came through.

Bednar made one other lineup change, bringing in Nicolas Aube-Kubel in place of Andre Burakovsky, who appeared to injure himself while blocking an Evan Bouchard shot in Game 1. The coach declined to say whether Burakovsky was hurt or a healthy scratch — "I'm not gonna tell you lineup decisions or injuries," he said — but the winger was seen walking with a noticeable limp earlier in the day. A lower-body injury feels like a safe assumption.

Throughout the evening, the Oilers tried to ramp up physicality on Colorado's stars, primarily MacKinnon and defenseman Cale Makar. Duncan Keith tripped MacKinnon after a whistle in the first period, for example, and Kane got a roughing penalty for hitting Makar along the boards in the third.

"You have to stand up for yourself a little bit, too, and show that you're here," Rantanen said. "I think that's what we did today. But obviously, we have to stay disciplined and stay out of the box and not be stupid."

Colorado happily took the power plays, and with Kane in the box, the Avalanche's two biggest stars teamed up for a goal to end any hope of an Oilers comeback. Makar fed MacKinnon, who beat a gloveless Smith to make it 4-0.

That capped arguably the Avalanche's most complete showing in the playoffs. They allowed only 11 shots in the final 40 minutes, making life smooth for Francouz. Unlike in Game 1, they didn't let the Oilers back in the game.

"I think that was what our group needed, the way to play in the third period there," Manson said. "We talked about it in between (periods) and how we wanted to accomplish it, and so it was good to get out and get that result for us." ▬▬

A Commanding Win with a Big Loss

Avalanche Inch Closer to Cup but Lose Nazem Kadri

By Peter Baugh

JUNE 5, 2022

Avalanche coach Jared Bednar called it the most dangerous type of play in hockey.

Nazem Kadri was skating toward the boards Saturday night, having just tapped a puck around the back of the net, when Oilers forward Evander Kane lifted his stick and drove it into Kadri's back. Kadri went flying, his left arm hitting the boards hard. The center stayed down on the ice for around a minute, and the officials assessed Kane a five-minute major penalty.

"I think it's incumbent on the league to address this targeted hit on Nazem with an appropriate suspension," Kadri's agent, Darren Ferris, said in a statement released to The Athletic. "If they don't address such a serious and dangerously callous hit, shame on them."

After the game, a 4-2 Avalanche win that gave them a commanding 3-0 lead in the best-of-seven series, Bednar said Kadri will miss at least the remainder of the Western Conference final. It's unclear if he'll be out should Colorado make the Stanley Cup Final. If he can't return, the hit from Kane might well have marked the final play of his Avalanche career. He will be an unrestricted free agent this summer and, after a career-best season, will draw heavy interest from teams around the league.

"Those are the (hits) that kind of gives you the chills down your spine, and you're taught from a young age that you don't do that, especially in that distance from the boards," Avalanche captain Gabriel Landeskog said. "I don't know what else to say. I'm sure (the league) will take a look at it."

Said Bednar: "He puts him in headfirst from behind, eight feet from the boards. I'll leave it at that." Kadri was reportedly seen leaving the arena with a cast on his right arm.

Kane, meanwhile, maintained that he was just trying to do an effective job on the backcheck.

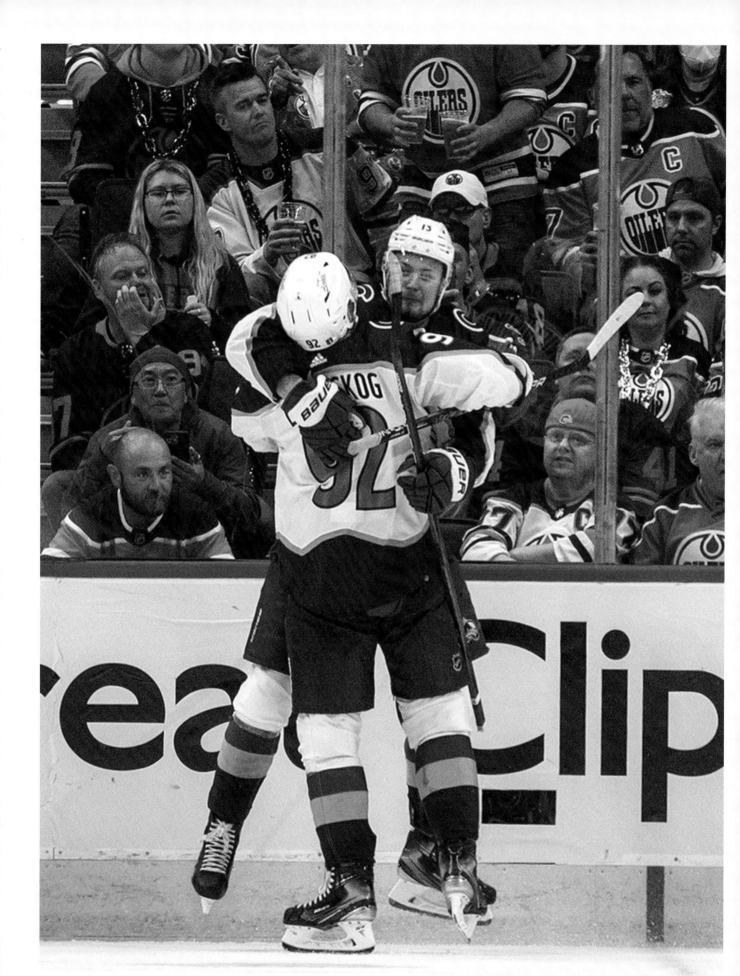

"Puck went wide, kind of dribbled into the corner," he said. "I know he likes to reverse it. I was just trying to get up on him, that's really all I did. Unfortunately, he went into the boards awkwardly."

Kadri's absence will leave a massive void for Colorado, and it puts a damper on a gutsy victory that leaves the Avalanche a win from the Stanley Cup Final. The center is coming off an 87-point regular season, and he has more than 100 points if you include the postseason. He was anchoring the second line with Mikko Rantanen and Artturi Lehkonen, a group that was playing at an elite level and contributed three goals in Game 3.

The Avalanche know how hard games can be without Kadri. Last season, his postseason suspension cost the team dearly, especially in the second-round series against Vegas. It forced forwards into roles they weren't ready for, and Colorado's struggling depth forwards were part of the reason the team blew a 2-0 series lead and lost four games in a row.

The Avalanche have a more complete team now than they did last postseason. They've prided themselves all postseason on their depth. But no one who plays at Kadri's level is waiting in the wings.

"His role will be filled by committee," Bednar said. "That's how big of a player he is for us. It could be one guy one night and a different guy the next. I'm comfortable with it. Obviously, it's a huge loss, but it's out of our control."

J.T. Compher will be one player who needs to step up, and he did in a major way Saturday after making what could have been a costly mistake. He tripped Leon Draisaitl midway through the third, then watched from the penalty box as goaltender Pavel Francouz robbed Connor McDavid with a glove save. Evan Bouchard nearly scored from outside, but the puck hit the post, keeping the 2-2 tie intact.

As Compher came out of the box, he beat Bouchard to an Andrew Cogliano pass, then charged toward Oilers goaltender Mike Smith. He tried to go between the netminder's legs but initially thought he'd failed when he saw Smith's positioning. He continued toward the net, looking for a rebound, then raised his hands in elation when he saw the puck in the back of the net.

"Definitely a roller coaster," Compher said of going from the penalty box to the goal. "Not a good time to take a penalty. Unbelievable job by our penalty kill, by Frankie. Little bit of luck off the post. Our penalty kill is doing a good job of limiting chances, and I can't thank that unit enough.

"From the lowest and in the box and waiting, and then being able to get one, that's the highs, for sure."

The goal stood after a strong defensive effort by the Avalanche's top players, who executed a five-on-six kill with Edmonton's net empty. Artturi Lehkonen and Devon Toews picked up key blocks, and Rantanen intercepted a Draisaitl pass and put it in the empty net with 30 seconds left to end any hopes of an Edmonton comeback.

"It shows you the kind of commitment you need to win games," said superstar center Nathan MacKinnon, who had an assist and a plus-two rating on the night. "If those pucks get through, who knows, right? The commitment that guys have in the room sacrificing themselves, playing for one another, and obviously Mikko, awesome reads. ... Great sacrifice from guys to get that win."

Most of the talk after the game, though, centered on Kadri's injury. Along with Compher, Alex Newhook and Nico Sturm could have to step up at center. Bednar could also shift Rantanen from wing to center, a position he played at points this season. If Andre Burakovsky, a capable goal scorer, can return from a suspected lower-body injury, he could also give the Avalanche a boost.

"We'll have to rethink things, see where our health is at with all of our guys," Bednar said. "Then pick a lineup that we think can get the job done here against the Oilers in Game 4." ■■■

Feel the Joy

Avalanche Have Embraced the Journey All the Way to the Stanley Cup Final

By Peter Baugh

JUNE 7, 2022

You don't have to wait until the pinnacle to feel the joy. The Avalanche are going to the Stanley Cup Final, and that's a big deal. Feel it, soak it in, celebrate.

No, the job isn't done. This is a team with bigger goals. But as Nathan MacKinnon said after the game, it's important to enjoy the journey. His team has a chance to win a championship, and that's an accomplishment in itself.

The players seemed to recognize that in the moments after finishing a sweep of the Oilers with a 6-5 win. There was the hyper-focused MacKinnon, who grinned, helmet unstrapped, as he walked from the ice to the dressing room. There was rookie Bowen Byram, who screamed, "Fuckin' right!" before throwing his arms around skills coach Shawn Allard. And there was 34-year-old Erik Johnson, the longest-tenured Denver athlete, whose eyes grew damp in his postgame news conference, reflecting on his 857-game journey in the NHL that has, at long last, led him to a Stanley Cup Final.

"You never know if that opportunity is going to come," he said.

But it did.

MacKinnon — who came to Colorado with the burden of expectation and has met everyone's, except maybe his own — is going to the Stanley Cup Final.

Captain Gabriel Landeskog — who acknowledged after the game that, in a dismal 2016-17 season, he doubted whether the Avalanche core would ever reach this point — is going to the Stanley Cup Final.

Cale Makar — who scored five points in the clinching Game 4 and whom Wayne Gretzky called the best player on the ice in every game of a series featuring Connor McDavid — is going to the Stanley Cup Final.

Forwards Mikko Rantanen and J.T. Compher, who were with the Avalanche at their lowest in 2017. Valeri Nichushkin and Jack Johnson, who came to Colorado hoping for a chance. Pavel Francouz, the No. 2 goalie who found a way to win four games in the conference final. They're all going to the Stanley Cup Final.

So is coach Jared Bednar, whom the Avalanche hired despite his lack of NHL experience. He'd never played at the highest level and hadn't even been an assistant in the league before general manager Joe Sakic gave him a chance, impressed by how he grinded in the minors, honing his craft, working for an opportunity. Sakic stuck with the coach after the 48-point 2016-17 disaster, and he stuck with him again after three consecutive second-round playoff exits.

"I wasn't in a rush to get to the NHL," Bednar said. "I'd still be coaching today if I was in the ECHL or the American League, but the opportunities came and I wanted to make sure I was ready. I put a lot of work into that and a lot of growth over the last few years, no question. Not unlike our team.

"I'm just one piece to it — I'm just one piece to it. It's been a lot of fun, and we're going to get a heck of an opportunity here."

Sakic rode the elevator down after the game with assistant general manager Chris MacFarland, who helped build a star-studded roster that managed to keep its depth. The Avs traded for Nazem Kadri, Devon Toews and Andre Burakovsky in previous offseasons, then made four additions at this year's deadline. One was depth forward Nico Sturm, who assisted a Makar overtime winner against Nashville in the first round. Another was Josh Manson, who scored an overtime winner against the Blues. A third was forward Andrew Cogliano, who has chipped in two game-winning goals this postseason.

But front and center Monday night was Artturi Lehkonen, whom Sakic acquired from Montreal for former first-rounder Justin Barron and a second-round pick. The forward grabbed a rebound in front of the net less than two minutes into overtime and made sure it was on his stick. Then, after what Makar said felt like a full minute, he fired it past a sprawling Mike Smith.

Game over, series over.

"That's why you trade for guys like that at the deadline," MacKinnon said. "I'd trade 10 first-rounders for him right now."

It wasn't the first time Lehkonen has come through in a big moment. Playing for the Canadiens last season, he scored a conference final overtime winner against Vegas to send his team to the Cup Final.

"Chance to play for the Stanley Cup doesn't come very often," he said after the game. "You've got to make the most of it. This year is an opportunity for us."

Colorado's stars showed up in the final game, with MacKinnon, Landeskog, Rantanen and Toews all scoring. But Makar, the first player to put the puck in the net Monday, shined brightest of all. He's up to 22 points in 14 games this postseason, all while taking on hard defensive assignments and continually coming through.

"We're lucky," Erik Johnson said, "because we're watching greatness."

The Avalanche showed a comfort level playing from behind that they sometimes lacked last season, when they won the Presidents' Trophy for the best regular-season record but fizzled against Vegas in the playoffs. Colorado trailed 3-1 entering the third period, then 4-2. But the Avs clawed back and took the lead with five minutes left, only to give it back moments later.

The prospect of a late blown lead didn't faze Bednar's bunch, though. Johnson said the team went into the locker room after regulation believing all the pressure was on Edmonton. Avalanche players knew from experience: They'd blown a multi-goal lead in Game 5 of their second-round series with the Blues, losing in overtime. This time they turned the tables.

"We've been up and we've gotten tight," MacKinnon said. "We figured, 'Let's make these guys tight. Put a little doubt in their mind.' Their season was on the line, and we pushed and pushed, and we finally broke through."

Added Bednar: "There's been a lot of growth, even from last season and the heartbreak we've had over the last couple of years, to be as resilient as we've been."

The Avalanche have reached their first Stanley Cup Final since 2001, and they've done so by eliminating key players from past eras. First was Nashville's Matt Duchene, who, by his own request, was traded in 2017. Then was St. Louis' Ryan O'Reilly, who was moved in a 2015 trade with Buffalo. And now has come Edmonton's Tyson Barrie, a dressing room favorite who was moved in Sakic's 2019 deal to acquire Kadri. Barrie walked through the handshake line after the game, warmly greeting his old friends in defeat.

In the moments after shaking hands, NHL deputy commissioner Bill Daly presented Landeskog with the Clarence Campbell Bowl, given to the Western Conference winners. Landeskog didn't touch the trophy at first (some consider it bad luck), but when MacKinnon came over, both put their hands on it — two of the team's leaders celebrating a new height reached.

The players didn't pick up the bowl, though. That celebration, if it happens, will have to wait for the Stanley Cup, still four wins away.

"Hopefully, we go out and put our best foot forward and go win the thing," Bednar said.

As players repeated, the job isn't finished. Far from it. But that doesn't mean the journey isn't one to savor. ▬▬

This book is available in quantity at special discounts for your group or organization.
For further information, contact:

Triumph Books LLC
814 North Franklin Street
Chicago, Illinois 60610
Phone: (312) 337-0747
www.triumphbooks.com

Printed in U.S.A.
ISBN: 978-1-63727-246-6

The Athletic

Paul Fichtenbaum, Chief Content Officer
Dan Kaufman, Editorial Director
Chris Sprow, Editorial Director
Evan Parker, SVP/GM Content Operations
James Mirtle, Senior Managing Editor - NHL
Aron Yeomanson, Managing Editor - NHL
Jake Leonard, Deputy Managing Editor - NHL
Rich Hammond, Senior Editor - NHL
Oscar Murillo, VP Design
Wes McCabe, Design Director
Kenny Dorset, Social Engagement
Trevor Gibbons, Partnerships Director
Jenna Winchell, Marketing Director
Casey Malone, Associate CRM Director
Amanda Ephrom, Brand Strategist
Tyler Sutton, Marketing Manager
Ankur Chawla, Business Development
Brooks Varni, Editorial Operations
Rosalie Pisano, Partnerships Manager
Emma Lingan, Programming Manager
Christy Aumer, Marketing Operations

Featured writers from The Athletic
Peter Baugh, Sean Gentille

Special thanks to the entire The Athletic NHL Staff

Content packaged by Mojo Media, Inc.
Joe Funk: Editor
Jason Hinman: Creative Director